Bob Buckley
Spring
'91

MASTERING
TECHNICAL
WRITING

MASTERING TECHNICAL WRITING

Joseph C. Mancuso

Addison-Wesley Publishing Company

Reading, Massachusetts Menlo Park, California New York
Don Mills, Ontario Wokingham, England Amsterdam Bonn
Sydney Singapore Tokyo Madrid San Juan

Library of Congress Cataloging-in-Publication Data

Mancuso, Joseph C.
  Mastering technical writing / Joseph C. Mancuso.
    p. cm.
  ISBN 0-20152350-7
  1. Technical writing. I. Title.
T11.M336 1990
808'.0666--dc20   89-49582
                                             CIP

Many of the designations used by manufacturers and sellers to distinguish their products are claimed as trademarks. Where those designations appear in this book and Addison-Wesley was aware of a trademark claim, the designations have been printed in initial caps or all caps.

Sponsoring editor, Ted Buswick
Production Supervisor, Perry McIntosh
Cover design by Lynne Reed
Text design by Joyce Weston
Set in 10 point Optima by Context Publishing Services

ABCDEFGHIJ—MW—9543210
First Printing, April 1990

Dedication

To my darlings, Sara and Andrew Mancuso.

. . . Love alters not with his brief hours and weeks,
But bears it out even to the edge of doom . . .

—*SHAKESPEARE, sonnet 116*

Daddy loves you, *always.*

CONTENTS

PART 2—PREPARING FOR THE TECHNICAL WRITING PROCESS

PART 3—THE TECHNICAL WRITING PROCESS

PART 4—REVISE THE DOCUMENT

ACKNOWLEDGMENTS

Charles P. Mancuso and Paul C. Mancuso, my brothers, for their advice, support, and regard.

Lino Stanchich, my teacher, for showing me the path to greater productivity.

Bob Nieman, my editor, for lending his creativity.

Ted Buswick, Addison-Wesley Product Development Manager, for offering enthusiasm for this project and for meeting the deadlines we set.

The members of the Society for Technical Communication, Lone Star Chapter, for their advice and camaraderie.

My colleagues at Texas Instruments for their fellowship.

PREFACE

Mastering Technical Writing (MTW) emphasizes the nine stages of a technical writing process (TWP). This particular version of a TWP works for me and the students I have taught.

You may use MTW as a self-paced course, reading it from cover-to-cover, or you may treat it as a reference work, dipping into it when questions arise in your writing tasks.

Whether you take one approach or the other, you may depend on MTW's ability to help you identify essential writing problems and remedies.

MTW "digs in" where the problems are—with writing style and organization. The text painstakingly shows why passive voice, weak verbs, jargon, and unnecessary words negatively affect the clarity of documents, and then shows how technical communicators may identify and remedy these offending constructions.

MTW offers technical communicators a tool kit for their documents. It supplies "wrenches" and "screwdrivers" for writing style, and "hammers" and "saws" for organizing documents. MTW furnishes hands-on information—immediate solutions to real-world documentation problems.

1

Introduction to Mastering Technical Writing

CONTENTS

Welcome to MTW

Who Can Profit from This Book?

Anyone who writes and reads technical documents can profit from reading Mastering Technical Writing (MTW). This book is designed to demonstrate techniques that can help you write concise and organized documents that appeal to particular audiences.

When you finish reading MTW, you will be able to write clearer documents—and you'll be able to write them faster and more easily.

What You Will Learn

When you finish this introduction to MTW, you will know

* Who MTW is meant to serve
* Why technical writing is not an easy subject to teach
* Many of the typical documentation problems in business
* Ideas to keep in mind as you go through MTW
* The teaching approach and format of MTW.

About MTW

The Increasing Role of Technical Communicators

More and more engineering reports are written, beginning to end, by engineers without benefit of inputs from a technical publications department. This trend is growing for two reasons. First, the cost of having a technical publications group oversee all engineering writing at a particular company is prohibitive. Second, as engineers, computer scientists, and other technical personnel increase their publishing capabilities with word processing packages, desktop publishing software, and laser printers, they are more able to produce their own documents.

An Aid for All Writers

MTW is designed to aid writers who begin and complete their own writing tasks. But it is also designed to help all technical communicators—regardless of where they fit into the documentation process.

Teaching Technical Writing

A Roadmap to Clear Writing

Before you read MTW, I want to tell you where you're going and how you're going to get there.

You will discard old attitudes and adopt new ones. You will examine specific writing problems and discover techniques to solve those problems. You will develop an organized, concise writing style that will allow you to enjoy your writing tasks. Also, you will be able to accomplish these tasks more quickly.

Unlearning Old Habits

MTW asks, "Can you teach an 'old' dog new tricks?" Can you, after so many years of schooling, unlearn the methods English teachers foisted on you in their attempts to teach you to write?

Technical writing is not easy to teach, and it does take time, because you need to unlearn what you've learned—the writing habits and rules that don't work. You're not starting from scratch—before you can learn new techniques and attitudes, you'll have to set aside your "knowledge" from the past.

EXERCISE MTW-1 (Individual)

List the problems you encounter when you are asked to write a document. These problems may relate to writing style, format, scheduling, or the like.

Typical Writing Problems in Business

11 Major Writing Problems

Within this book, we will "roll in the dust" with the following 11 major problems seen in technical documents:

1. Documents fail to fulfill the requirements of customers.
2. Documents fail to appeal to their audiences.
3. Writers fail to address the purposes of documents.
4. Writers take too long to write documents.
5. Documents are disorganized.
6. Writers use passive voice verbs that hide and distort the meaning of information.
7. Writers use weak, unfocused verbs that dilute the meaning of information.
8. Writers use jargon that hides the meaning of information.
9. Writers use too many words to convey too little meaning.
10. Writers write unprofessional appearing reports.
11. Documents contain unreadable, uninviting text.

A Few Thoughts to Consider

Keep These Ideas in Mind

Let me give you some clues about what's coming by asking you to keep these ideas in mind:

- Constantly put yourself in the reader's place. Do everything possible to smooth the way for your reader.
- We should read technical writing, not decipher it.
- Less is more. The less you tax a reader's concentration, the more the reader will understand your message. Say what you *must* say and get off stage.
- Write as you speak—at least in the first draft of your message. As much as possible, let the reader hear your conversational voice in your writing.
- Think about what you will say and then organize your message. Your organizational scheme should make it difficult for readers to misunderstand your message.
- Place the most important information at the beginning of sentences, paragraphs, and sections.

- Enhance clarity by expressing all, or most, sentences in a natural order—subject, predicate, object.
- Use strong, active verbs to promote meaning that leaps off the page.

The Technical Writing Process

Workshop Tools

MTW mixes lectures, discussions, and writing exercises to convey its lessons.

Preparing for the Technical Writing Process

MTW includes a segment (Part 2) called "Preparing for the Technical Writing Process." This segment is divided into four chapters:

1. Set Your Attitudes Straight
2. Understand the Waste Associated with Unclear Documents
3. Know What Technical Writing Is
4. Know How You Fit into the Documentation Process.

The Technical Writing Process

MTW is organized according to the Technical Writing Process (TWP), a system or procedure that leads you through the stages of writing documents. I have emphasized in MTW the following nine stages—representing the stages of the Technical Writing Process:

1. Understand the Requirements, Audience, and Purpose of Documents (Chapter 5)
2. Gather Information for the Document (Chapter 6)
3. Brainstorm the Information (Chapter 7)
4. Categorize the Information (Chapter 8)
5. Sort the Information (Chapter 9)
6. Outline the Information (Chapter 10)
7. Design the Document (Chapter 11)
8. Write the Document (Chapter 12)
9. Revise the Document (all of Part 4—Chapters 13–17).

You will not need to use each stage of the process each time you write a document. Depending on the assignment, you may omit stages or perform tasks in different sequences.

I will illustrate lessons in this book with passages from reports, proposals, and manuals. You will learn about effective technical writing style—techniques that will serve you *no matter what kinds of documents you write.*

MTW Format

How Each Chapter Is Organized

This book emphasizes nine stages (Chapters 5–17)—each representing a stage of TWP. In this book, each chapter is organized as follows:

- Table of Contents—A handy reference tool.
- Overview—A brief overview of the chapter and a look at the objectives for the chapter.
- Topics—The major topics that contain specific information related to each stage. For example, in this chapter, MTW Format is the current topic, and The Technical Writing Process was the previous topic. A major topic may include several subtopics.
- Summary—Closing remarks about the chapter.

Express Yourself

Speak Out and Enjoy

Welcome. Relax. Keep in mind the ideas I mentioned earlier. From now on, you will write less formally and use a process, the TWP, to write your documents. Also, think about "speaking" the first draft of your documents.

PART

2

Preparing for the Technical Writing Process

CONTENTS

Before You Begin...

Where Do You Stand?

Many of you already understand the inappropriate attitudes, learned in school and on the job, that contribute to ineffective technical writing. You also realize the waste that accompanies ineffective documents. Further, you know what technical writing is and how you fit into the overall documentation process.

For you, the information in "Preparing for the Technical Writing Process" is secondary; you may not need to read much of this information. For others, this preparatory information will ensure that you "buy in" to the principles espoused in MTW; you should read carefully each of the four chapters of "Preparing for the Technical Writing Process."

Four Key Parts

This segment consists of the following four chapters:

1. Set Your Attitudes Straight
2. Understand the Waste Associated With Unclear Documents
3. Understand What Technical Writing Is
4. Know How You Fit into the Documentation Process.

1 ·

Set Your Attitudes Straight

CONTENTS

Overcoming Learned Attitudes

The Root of Our Problems

Learned attitudes related to writing often destroy our confidence in our ability to write effectively. At the least, these attitudes undermine or lessen our ability to write effectively.

Overcoming these attitudes is a key to effective writing, since these attitudes are the root of the problem.

What You Will Learn

When you finish Chapter 1, you will know how to

- Identify inappropriate attitudes related to writing—learned in school and on the job
- Identify attitudes that can help you write more effectively and more easily.

Attitudes That Inhibit Technical Communicators

Stumbling Blocks

Before we discuss documentation problems and solutions, we must first identify attitudes that inhibit us as we write. These inappropriate attitudes toward writing constitute a larger problem, which relates to all the problems we will address in this book. We must identify these inappropriate attitudes and discard them, and then adopt appropriate attitudes that can assist us in writing effective documents. These appropriate attitudes are the *foundation techniques* we need to write clearly.

Writing Tasks Are Viewed as Drudgery

Unfortunately, many writers view their writing tasks as drudgery, as impersonal, get-it-over-with activities. *This attitude conflicts with what most documents really are—important messages that human beings depend on.*

Who Is at Fault?

Why do educated business and technical professionals produce impersonal, unclear documents? Why are the documents produced by most companies criticized as being unappealing, even unreadable? The answer is that professionals are poorly trained by our educational system and, later, by their employers.

> Interrupt your reading here. Do not read any further. Right now, work through Exercise 1-1.

EXERCISE 1-1 (Individual or Team)

Respond, as an individual or a team, to the following discussion topics. Record your responses on a notepad.

1. Describe who is at fault for our failure to write clearly, to communicate in ways that make sure our audiences really understand our messages.
2. Describe some attitudes that you learned in school and on the job that inhibit your ability to write as clearly as you would like.

Take 15 minutes to respond to these topics.

FAILURE to write clearly

> When you finish this exercise, read the related discussion on the following pages.

Traditional Teaching Vs. the Real World

Who teaches writing to whom? English teachers teach writing courses to students, who mostly go into business or technical fields. Have the English teachers been in business? Are they technical? Are the English teachers writers? Do they write every day and publish their works? "A few" is the answer to all four questions.

When I criticize English teachers, I am criticizing my "old" self, an unaware self whom colleagues in industry helped to shape.

Problems with Traditional Methods

Writing is not well taught for two reasons:

1. Many English teachers prepare themselves to teach writing by reading literature. Even though they may write a thesis and/or dissertation, *most English teachers are not writers.* Please don't misunderstand my intent. Some of the most enjoyable and meaningful hours of my life have been spent with instructors, analyzing poetry and prose and relating literature to my own experiences. English teachers are wonderfully qualified and dedicated to helping students with these important tasks. However, many English teachers do not have a first-hand understanding of writing processes, problems, and techniques. Writers who write every day and publish their works understand these matters.

2. English teachers use models that do not relate to the writing most students must do at their jobs. Most of the time students must "simply" communicate information.

An Example of Stilted Writing

I recently read a Department of English memorandum that contained the following sentence:

> It is obvious that this document will have to be amended from time to time as new duties arise and as present duties are altered in one fashion or the other.

The author, chairman of the department, wanted to say:

> We will amend this document as duties change.

But the author didn't know how to express his message concisely. No one pressured the author to deliver the message quickly and without waste.

"I'm Not Good Enough"

We're told from the time that we are young that we are inadequate: We don't play sports well; we don't do enough work around the house; we are not attractive enough to interest members of the opposite sex; and we don't write well.

In our writing efforts, we are clearly and demonstrably inadequate. Our subjects and verbs don't agree; we fail to use the nominative and objective cases of pronouns properly; our sentences are awkward; our items in a series are not parallel; and so on. English teachers show us often just how inadequate we are.

We internalize this inadequacy and become inhibited. We tighten up. *Our prose becomes formal, stilted.* Our writing no longer reflects us as persons because no one wants to place an inadequate person into his/her prose. We distance ourselves from our subjects. We use canned language whenever possible because that language is accepted.

Unlearning "Bad" Attitudes

Learning to write is a "shrinking" process. It is a process of identifying learned attitudes and then unlearning them. We need to climb up on the "shrink's" couch and resolve those conflicts related to writing.

Attitudes from Educational Experiences

An Agenda for Unlearning

In the following discussions, I'm going to state the new attitude I want you to adopt first. Underneath the new attitude, I'll state the old, inappropriate attitude in parentheses and italics.

The Grammar Trap

More Than Just Grammar

Writing Is Chiefly Problem Solving
(The most important aspects of writing are grammatical, mechanical.)

The emphasis in writing should be on problem solving, planning, and organizing. Some of my early teachers briefly addressed planning and organizing; none ever talked about problem solving. My teachers emphasized the mechanical aspect of writing—"Write *whom*, not *who*," or "Use *I*, not *me*."

Let me tell you about the 2,000-year-old man as played by Mel Brooks. He knew everyone in history, even Shakespeare, whom he called "a terrible writer." When asked why Shakespeare was a terrible writer, the 2,000-year-old man replied, "Look at Shakespeare's manuscripts. They're filled with ink blots and scratchings, and his penmanship was terrible!" The old man, like too many English teachers, emphasized the mechanical aspects of writing.

What's the Problem?

Writing is problem solving. For instance, I recently encountered the following problem—"How do I make notes for myself, as an instructor, to prompt me while I discuss points with workshop participants? I want the notes close at hand so that I can follow the discussion in the participant's manual and elaborate on that discussion." I solved the problem by creating "Instructor's Notes," loose-leaf additions to the participant's manual, which I place in my own copy of the participant's manual.

"Instructor's Notes" need not be formatted carefully or tidied up because I'm the only one who will see them. Also, I can write them in a shorthand style and use jargon that I understand. I solved a personal teaching problem, and the solution keyed the style and substance of my document.

A Typical Scenario

You go through the same process in writing your documents. You solve problems. For instance, you experience a problem on the assembly line—manufactured widgets are not holding to the required specifications. You must find out why. You need to communicate the problem to the employees responsible for design and manufacturing. You could call them individually on the phone, but you need a record of your communication and you need to communicate more efficiently than calling 10 staff members and discussing the problem with them individually. You decide to write a report in the form of a memo. Now you know the form your communication will take and you know the substance of the memo. How about the style? Since you know your audience—you have worked with them for years—you will write a technically accurate but informal memo. So now you have the tone for the memo. And the hatching of your plans for this memo proceeds.

Beware of "Expert" Advice

Experts Don't Have All the Answers

Don't Mimic the Style of "Experts" in the Field
(Study the Style of Particular Authors and Follow Their Style)

Throughout their academic lives and on into their business careers, engineers read textbooks and journal articles written by experts. Unfortunately, the experts have learned the same lessons of style—to use passive voice, weak verbs, and nominals[*] that perpetuate the writing of unclear documents. Further, the experts fail to flesh their ideas out sufficiently for less informed audiences.

The Arrogant Writer

"Arrogant" authors tend to create new words. Creating new words isn't bad in itself; however, these newly created words—understood only by the author or by a few others—will confound most audiences. For instance, consider the verb *perturb:* "Receiver thermal noise *perturbs* the incoming signal." There is also the noun *perturbation*: "Major *perturbations* of the input produce large variations in the output." But the neologism, or new word, *perturbate*, does not exist, as in "We will *perturbate* the sequence of data samples to ensure statistical independence."

Apply the same thinking to the words *console, consolation, consolate.* There's no such animal as *consolate.*

Personalized Writing

Be Yourself When You Write

Inject Your Own Personality into Your Writing
(Do Not Use the First Person Pronoun Excessively)

Avoiding the first person is one of the first steps on the road to doubting our own importance in the writing process.

When teachers caution not to use too many "I's" in your text, what are they saying? First, they're saying, "Keep your prose impersonal." We may understand that to mean that the subject is more important than the writer. In a sense, this is true, but this impression inhibits us. We separate ourselves from the subject rather than interacting with the subject. Don't be afraid to project yourself in your writing.

---

[*] See Part 4 to understand these writing style problems.

Point of View

Point of view is the personal or impersonal attitude you exhibit toward your audience as reflected in your use of personal pronouns such as *I, we, you,* and *they.*

By using the third person pronoun (*he, she, it, they*), or a noun standing in the place of a third person pronoun (e.g., *the team*), you can achieve an impersonal point of view: "It will be finished by August 1," or "The report will be finished by August 1." By using the first person pronoun (*I, we*), you can achieve a personal point of view: "I (we) will finish the report by August 1." By using the second person pronoun (*you*), you can also achieve a personal point of view, this time spotlighting the audience rather than the writer: "You will finish the report by August 1."

How Point of View Can Improve Your Writing

Historically, technical people have used the impersonal point of view because they thought it made writing sound more objective and professional. However, the impersonal point of view often obscures communication, as illustrated in the following example:

Introduction

As part of an Effectiveness Team Inquiry, it was desired to determine the maximum allowable quantity of gold deposits in resistor areas. For the first seven months of 1986, 2576 detector ceramics were scrapped due to gold in the resistor area. This computes to an annual scrap cost of 74.3K. Through a concerted effort of the Ceramics Photogenics ET, the annual scrap rate based on fourth quarter '86 data, was reduced to 16.5K. Most of this reduction resulted from process, inspection, and handling improvements, while the remainder came from increased inspection time. The reduction of this increased manufacturing inspection time as well as the removal of the remaining rejects are the objectives of this inquiry.

Working with the above example, you can achieve a personal point of view to communicate the same information more clearly and still adhere to the purpose of the document:

You asked us, the Effectiveness Team (ET), to determine the maximum allowable quantity of gold deposits in resistor areas. In order to do this, we inquired about the inspection time and removal of remaining rejects.

A New Rule to Follow

We fear using the personal point of view because English teachers discouraged us from using *I, me*, etc. New rule: Don't be afraid to use the more personal point of view (the first person) in your reports. The personal point of view does not detract from your message.

What difference does it make to your audience whether "I's" pepper the text if the required information is there?

Short Sentences

Stick with Short Sentences

Keep Most of Your Sentences Short
(Vary the Length of Your Sentences)

Teachers taught me to write long sentences interspersed with short ones. They talked about pace. I guess pace is important to a musical composition, a poem, and fiction, but not when we communicate straight information. If short sentences communicate crisply, use short sentences.

Infuse short sentences with one, well-thought-out idea and arrange these short sentences in a logical pattern. Make it difficult for the audience to misinterpret what you say.

Say It Straight

Stick with Simple Sentences

Write Most of Your Sentences in Natural Word Order
(Vary the Word Order of Your Sentences)

Subject-verb-object is the natural word order: "I kicked the ball," not "The ball was kicked by me." Studies show that audiences process information most effectively when authors present sentences in the natural pattern. Yet teachers still urge student authors to use introductory words, phrases, or clauses; to invert the order of clauses; and to vary the patterns of words within sentences.

Instead, let your sentences march along in subject-verb-object word order, and leave variety to those audiences more impressed with "the bells and whistles" of language. Again, make it difficult for your audience to misunderstand your message. Deliver your message in a simple, straightforward manner. No one ever read a report and said, *"I'm sorry. This is too easy for me to understand."*

Keep It Simple

Watch Your Languange

Use the More Readily Understood Word Whenever Possible
(Use "Big" Words)

I get a big kick out of William Buckley, the author, publisher, and news analyst. He "cut his teeth" on Latin and Greek and, as a result, knows the English language intimately. He specializes in using words like *ratiocinate* (to think)—a wonderful word derived from the Latin. Buckley's problem, though, is that he uses these "big" words regardless of his audience, caring little about whether or not the audience understands them. Buckley once used *ratiocinate* on Muhammad Ali, and Ali almost fell over with laughter. Ali took it good-naturedly, but I'm sure that Buckley seeks to intimidate most of his audiences.

The "bigger" the words, the more "professional," "technical," and "scientific" we sound. When we use unfamiliar "big" words, we take another step on the journey toward doubting our own importance in the writing process. The journey leads to

- Writer's block, a paralysis in which we cringe at the thought of exposing ourselves on the blank page
- Stilted writing, in which we use passive voice, poor diction, and long, convoluted sentences to express ideas.

Keep It Short

Don't Pad Your Writing

Less Is More
(Fill Up the Page)

My teachers conveyed the impression that the more we wrote, the more "weight" we added to our efforts, and the better our grades would be. Filling up the page indicated a solid effort. I wonder where the joke originated that had students sticking their old math homework into their book reports and receiving a high grade from the teacher for their efforts.

We learn to stretch our prose. Instead of saying, "The children played," a social scientist might say, "The children were put in a play situation."

Say what you have to say, and get off stage. Don't pad your writing with unnecessary information or words.

Selective Repetition

Don't Be Afraid to Repeat

Repeat Nouns to Avoid Ambiguity
(Do Not Repeat the Same Word)

Again, for the sake of variety, teachers encouraged us not to repeat the same words. They encouraged us to go to the thesaurus and find synonyms. For instance, I remember a teacher rhapsodizing over Shakespeare's rich and varied use of language. One could examine many lines from his plays and not see words repeated. I suppose the same teachers would have us alternate *report* with *document* and *text* for the sake of richness and variety in a progress report. This is not necessary. In fact, it may suggest ambiguity to the audience, causing the audience to wonder whether or not the writer is referring to the same piece of writing.

A major error in technical documents occurs when writers substitute a pronoun for an "overworked" noun. Often, the pronoun inaccurately refers to its antecedent, forcing the audience to "decipher" the author's meaning.

The Transition Trap

Strive to Write Logically

Organize Information as Tightly as Possible
(Use Transitional Words)

Oh, how I loved *moreover, further, finally*, and *with regard to*. They bridged my thoughts—but not well. They provided me with a crutch: I avoided the need to tightly organize my thoughts according to a careful, logical arrangement. Poorly organized language demands the use of many transitional words. Logically placed details flow smoothly and do not require elaborate transitional phrases.

Titles That Talk

Make Your Headings Useful

Use Action Titles
(Use Headings Like Introduction, Body, and Conclusion)

Many headings say little about the text that follows, other than "this text begins the report" (Introduction), "this text resides in the middle of the report" (Body), or "this text concludes the report" (Conclusion).

Sections of a report need descriptive headings. We should use action titles for headings wherever possible, working in the titles of companies, products, problems, solutions, and methods—thereby alerting the reader to the content of the text and not simply its position in the report. Instead of *Introduction,* use *Four Methods to Change a Spare Tire,* for example, to begin a manual.

Don't Delay Your Message

First Things First

Place Important Information at the Front of the Document
(Documents Need Conclusions)

I could never understand the logic of writing a conclusion for the typical three-paragraph, one-page theme. The audience would need to suffer severe memory loss to forget important points the author made in the previous two paragraphs. While I agree with the wisdom that encourages writers to tell and then retell information, there is a point of diminishing or nonexistent returns.

One problem with conclusions is that authors save important details for the conclusion—information never mentioned in the beginning or body of the report. When the author puts the most important information at the end of the document, it is because the author has finally figured out what he/she wants to say at the end of the document.

The reverse should be true. Writers should carefully plan and outline their documents and know what the document will reveal *before* they write. That way they can position the most important information in the introduction.

Don't Be Afraid to Fail

Mistakes Are Part of the Process

Show Your Ignorance—Ignorance Is Required
(Ignorance Is Bad, Mistakes Are Bad)

Why do we quake even today at the thought of asking questions in front of an audience? We are apprehensive, frightened to "display our ignorance." We're supposed to be smart; in fact, we're supposed to know *everything,* or so we've been led to believe by teachers, who chide us for our inability to regurgitate all the facts.

Why do we edit ourselves mercilessly as we try to write? Can't you just see yourself checking each word that you write for diction, spelling, number, case, gender, *ad infinitum*. We're afraid to make a mistake. Mistakes are bad. Teachers spill red ink all over papers that contain mistakes.

This kind of up-tight writing results in paralysis. We avoid the writing task. We perform only when some university requires us to suffer a writing course or some manager separates us from our "real" tasks and forces us to document our work. ("Where are the technical writers—the guys who get paid for this stuff!")

The Paper Myth

Paper Lets Us Communicate

Paper Is Only a Vehicle for Communicating Our Messages
(Paper Is Sacred)

I used to imagine that my English teachers carried our graded papers on a velvet pillow as though they carried a crown. I imagined a kind of religious aura around the event of writing. Today, I tell students that I intend to keep all of their papers in my vault and that someday I will meet them on the street as they walk with someone they are trying to impress, and I will pull out all their old papers and shout to everyone within earshot how stupid they were for writing so poorly.

Paper is only a vehicle for the spoken word. At some point in our history, the oral tradition began to erode, and we began to use paper to record our thoughts and to send our messages to far-off places. We never intended for communicators to revere paper and treat it as any more than a means to convey oral messages.

Writing Is Your Job

Everyone's a Writer

Almost Everyone Should Be Prepared to Write on the Job
(Only Professional Writers Write on the Job)

I never suspected that secretaries, nurses, attorneys, executives, and engineers spent much of their professional lives documenting their work. As far as I knew, writers were bearded, offbeat characters who traveled the world and wrote novels in bohemian garrets and on exotic islands. They wrote stories, not proposals and manuals. Yes, I knew that some corrupted, commercial hacks wrote advertising copy and brochures for companies, but I looked on them with the same disdain I harbored for artists who illustrated commercial products.

Good Writing Makes Business Work

My teachers should have explained the valuable role business writers and commercial artists play in disseminating information about technological advances. Teachers should have pointed out, too, just how much writing we all do during our careers and should have exhorted us to learn to write technically—before we were forced to learn on the job.

Unfortunately, technical writers and editors are not paid their due on the job. Many people still consider technical writing a slight cut above the clerical function.

Know Your Reader

Don't Write to Please "Experts"

We Write for Many Audiences—and We Must Know Them
(Only One Audience Exists)

For 16 years, through college and beyond, students write for one audience—their instructors—and never learn to vary their verbal appeal. Engineers, of course, must communicate with many audiences—fellow engineers, technicians, managers, technical and nontechnical government employees, etc.—and must be conversant with the techniques that appeal to these audiences.

The Importance of Planning

Get Ready—Then Write

Outline Your Documents
(Preparing to Write Is Not Important)

When I talk to English instructors about preparing to write, they reiterate the importance of topic and topic sentence outlines. Somehow, the importance of outlining is rarely transferred to students. For six years, I polled my university classes each semester and asked which students outlined before they wrote. Out of 25 students in each class, perhaps two or three said that they outlined before writing. The same holds true when I poll veteran writers in corporate seminars. In both settings, the naysayers respond sheepishly, leading me to believe that instructors have encouraged outlining but have never sold it.

Attitudes from the Workplace

Overcoming Business Attitudes

Just as attitudes from our educational experience hamper our ability to communicate clearly, attitudes developed in the workplace limit us as we strive to complete our tasks successfully. Below are some of the new attitudes we want to adopt, with the corresponding "old" attitudes in italics.

Get Started Quickly

The Early Bird . . .

Begin to Document as Early as Possible
(Write Documentation at the End of the Cycle)

Companies believe in the primary importance of product development. Developing products begins with initiatives from clients or from staff within. These initiatives proceed to research and development phases and, ultimately, to production. Unfortunately, documentation usually begins *after* the production phase of product development—and this delay in documenting usually results in inferior documents and less effective products.

Why the Delays?

Why do companies delay producing documents? First, companies do not realize the importance of clear documents. Though companies have recently realized that attractive, intelligible documents can help sell their products, companies still do not recognize the most important reason for beginning the documentation process, even before the research phase of product development—to produce more effective hardware/software products.

Also, documentation, written from the beginning, affects the marketing of a product by demonstrating what the product can do for particular clients—not what the marketing department hopes the product can do for multi-markets.

Allow Time for Good Documentation

Deadlines Should Be Realistic

Clear Documentation Takes Time
(Staff Can Produce Documentation Very Quickly)

Companies often set unrealistic deadlines for production of documentation. When I started my first writing job, managers told me that I could accomplish my documentation tasks very quickly—one boss wanted me to produce the corporate newsletter, complete with photos, drawings, and text, in two hours on a Friday afternoon. As it turned out, the job took Friday, most of Saturday, and part of Monday.

Because most companies have not, historically, respected the role of documentation in the total development effort, project managers allow minimal time for documentation. When companies remove their blinders and see that effective documentation creates readable documents *and* more effective products, then managers will allot sufficient time for the preparation of effective documents.

Technical Writing Is a Skill

Give Technical Writers Their Due

Writing Clear Documents Takes Great Skill
(Documentation is a "Clerical" Function)

Many executives and managers perceive documentation as a matter of "crossing t's and dotting i's." As you'll see throughout this book, documenting is far more than "crossing t's and dotting i's." The craft of writing, when practiced effectively, demands high-level skills.

Get the Skills You Need

Learn from "Real" Writers

If I wanted to learn to play tennis, I would not hire a coach who had read every book on tennis but had never stepped on a court to play. I would hire a coach who had played often and well.

The same thinking applies to writing.

Writers should teach writing to develop attitudes and skills in learners based on writers' successes and failures in appealing to audiences.

Review Attitudes Before Beginning Each Stage

At the beginning of each stage of the Technical Writing Process, I will suggest that you review one or more of the attitudes discussed in this chapter. For instance, in Stage 1 (Chapter 5), I ask you to review the following attutudes:

- Writing is problem-solving.
- Almost everyone should be prepared to write on the job.
- We write for many audiences—and we must know them.

2

Understand the Waste Associated with Unclear Documents

CONTENTS

Garbage In, Garbage Out

A Terrible Waste

Unclear technical documents represent a waste of a company's resources and profits. The company and its employees lose when proposals fail to attract business, when manuals fail to correctly describe operations of products, and when reports fail to document the business of projects.

The following pages show specifically how unclear documents waste resources.

What You Will Learn

When you finish Chapter 2, you will know those areas where a company can conserve and even enhance its resources by producing clear documents.

The Cost of Unclear Documents

Some Facts and Figures

A December 1987 article in *Personnel Journal* states that white-collar workers spend 21–70 percent of all working hours on paperwork. The article, titled "How to Slash the $100 Billion Cost of Paperwork," says that

- Americans create 30 billion original documents annually.
- Paperwork costs more than $100 billion in the United States each year.
- People ignore 75–85 percent of all documents they retain.
- American businesses maintain 18,000 pages (or a four-drawer file cabinet) of paper for each white-collar employee; this file size increases 4,000 pages per year for each employee.
- Excessive paperwork leads to dips in employee morale because most people view paperwork, or documentation, as drudgery.

The Role of Documentation

To prepare ourselves to write and edit competently, we must realize what the failure to write clear documents can cost a company. We do not write in a vacuum. What we write affects the lives of our audiences and colleagues.

> Stop reading now, and work through Exercise 2-1.

**EXERCISE 2-1
(Individual or Team)**

Respond as an individual or a team to the following discussion topic. Record your responses on a notepad.

Describe ways companies waste dollars as a result of unclear documents.

Take 10 minutes to complete the exercise.

> When you finish the exercise, read the related discussion on the following pages.

Where Costs Are Lost

Inaccurate Assessment of Costs—Loss of Profits

When companies consider soliciting new business, they gauge profitability by breaking down the overall project into many tasks and subtasks. Various groups within companies report to a project manager on the costs to the company in human and raw resources. Faulty documentation of manpower needs and materials results in

- Overbidding on lucrative contracts and subsequent loss of the contracts
- Underbidding on contracts and subsequent inadequate profits or substantial losses.

Beginning engineers, especially, must be aware of the consequences when they produce inaccurate documentation for tasks associated with proposals.

Interruptions and Reduced Productivity

Users will have questions when they attempt to operate hardware and software. Effective user manuals will answer most of these questions; ineffective manuals will not answer questions and will force a company to question its authors about the veracity of the manuals. These interruptions—questions for engineers—take authors away from their tasks and cost dollars.

Training Takes Time

Field engineers are not trained instructors and, depending on the complexity of the product, clients may need trained instructors to orient them to the product. Instructors may travel to distant client companies for weeks of training; in other cases, representatives from client companies, at their expense or the contractor's expense, may need to travel to the contractor's facility to stay for days or weeks of training.

Certainly, companies that maintain small or large staffs of instructors must be getting the message: more good instruction can take place with effective documentation.

Writing Time

It doesn't necessarily follow that if you write fewer words, you write more quickly. Certainly it takes time to develop a concise prose style, but once done, skilled, veteran writers with an economical style may complete their tasks more efficiently. It is difficult to estimate what a team of efficient, economically minded communicators saves a company, but it would be reasonable for companies that produce less-effective documents to add up the hours spent on documentation annually and then to deduct *one-third* of those hours as wasted time.

Lost Boilerplate—"Reinventing the Wheel"

When I began working as a technical writer with a Dallas/Fort Worth company, I asked whether or not the company captured boilerplate, or generic information, on its mainframe computer. The company did not. Technical writers "reinvented the wheel" for each specification, report, and manual—even though these documents used the same generic paragraphs year in and year out. What a waste of time and energy. It doesn't take much to imagine the enormous savings possible when writers can "plug in" boilerplate company history, resumé information, quality assurance steps, and other information that remains relatively stable from year to year.

Reading Time

Perhaps the most significant losses from ineffective documents occur in the hours audiences spend trying to decipher these documents. Let's say that a company produces an ineffective user manual for the hardware it sells. Let's say that the company sells 10,000 of the products in one year. Ten thousand users will read their manuals, to one extent or another, in order to operate their hardware. Would it be fair to say that two hours of reading time might be a mean? What fraction of those 20,000 hours served no useful purpose? Should we multiply the 20,000 by "x" number of companies throughout the world, producing similar products, accompanied by ineffective documents, to arrive at a final figure? How much are hundreds of thousands of wasted hours worth?

Personnel to Type, Collate, Fold, Mail, Etc.

The more bologna, the more staff needed to process it, slice it, package it, and deliver it. Ineffective, weighty documents—hundreds and thousands of pages long, sent to multitudes of consumers—demand more staff to disseminate them.

Paper, Postage, Storage Space

Larded, ineffective documents consume more paper, postage, and storage space. These dollars become significant when we consider storing and mailing thousands of weighty manuals and annual reports to thousands of users and, perhaps, millions of stockholders.

Reduce Your Waste Line

An Incalculable Loss

Unclear documents waste resources, and it is difficult to place a dollar figure on the waste. But the figure can be enormous.

If we consider only the waste of time devoted to deciphering ineffectual manuals and reports, we realize the sums that we can save by writing more effectively.

3

Understand What Technical Writing Is

CONTENTS

Technical Writing—A Closer Look

A Few Key Questions

You have seen technical documents. You know what they look like. But why do we produce them—beyond the utilitarian needs to attract business, describe the operation of products, and the like?

Also, what are some of the sources that can contribute to our in-depth understanding of why the technical documents are important and how we can more effectively produce them?

What You Will Learn

When you finish Chapter 3, you will

- Know more about the importance of technical documents
- Know resources to consult to learn more about the writing/editing of documents and about the profession of technical communication.

What Is Technical Writing?

Definition—Technical Writing

Technical writing is written communication that results in the production of documentation related to various kinds of hardware and software products, including computers and computer programs, industrial machinery, weaponry, and the like. These documents may be written by technical writers, engineers, computer analysts and programmers, scientists, and others. Technical writing occurs in industry and takes the form of memos, proposals, reports, manuals, specifications, and articles.

The Importance of Technical Writing

A Critical Skill

Technical writing facilitates the functioning of our economy through written communication among companies, their customers, and the public. Technical documents ensure the effective design, manufacture, and function of our country's critical defense systems.

A Foundation for Progress

Technical writing helps us do our jobs more easily. Because technical communicators document technology, we can avoid traveling paths others have already blazed. Technical documents furnish us with firm foundations for building new ideas and designs. For instance, we need not reinvent the Fast Fourier Transform (FFT) because it has been developed and documented. We also save development time by using documented information related to the higher functioning of systems and the radar equation; we also save time with documented processes used to make wafers and integrated circuits.

If we don't document in a form that others can build on, we lose ideas, and it is extremely costly to recapture these ideas.

Good Documentation Means a Quality Product

Technical personnel should realize the importance of documentation. They should see documentation as an integral part of product research and development—not as merely an adjunct to these functions.

When we can clearly describe products and their functions from the start of the developmental process, then we not only will produce quality documentation, but we also will produce more effective hardware and software.

Characteristics of Technical Writing

What Makes a Document "Technical"?

Technical documents are characterized by the following traits:

- They inform and persuade.
- They appeal to audiences with specific needs.
- They are written with specific purposes in mind.
- They are accurate because lives and dollars often depend on them.

Additional Characteristics

The aphorism, "Good writing is good writing, no matter what," is true, but technical documents can be distinguished from other

kinds of writing because technical documents contain the
following:

- Unambiguous language
- Data
- Graphics
- Varied formats
- Headings/action titles
- Acronyms.

Reference Sources for Technical Communicators

Four Current Resources

For assistance in writing clear documents and in teaching others to
write well, technical communicators can consult four excellent
journals in the field:

- *The Journal of Technical Writing and Communication*,
  published by Baywood Press for Rensselaer Polytechnic Institute
- *Technical Communication*, published by the Society for
  Technical Communication (STC)
- *The Technical Writing Teacher*, published by the Association of
  Teachers of Technical Writing (ATTW)
- *Transactions on Professional Communication*, published by the
  Institute for Electrical and Electronic Engineering (IEEE).

Finding the Resources

These journals are commonly available in college libraries.
Because they are periodicals, they contain current information.
The articles in the journals are usually a few pages long, and a
half-hour of reading time can provide important advice on a
particular topic.

Professional Organizations

What the Organizations Offer

Technical communicators can stay current in their field by
consulting journals and by joining professional organizations.
Professional organizations offer camaraderie and inside
information about jobs, trends, the latest technology, and valuable

continuing education opportunities. Attending meetings motivates communicators and instills pride in being part of the profession.

The Society for Technical Communication

The Society for Technical Communication (STC) is the field's premier organization. An international group of writers, editors, managers, and illustrators, the STC has chapters throughout the world, including major metropolitan areas of the United States.

The Benefits of Expertise

Technical writers who remain current in their profession can offer engineers and other technical staff the benefit of research and up-to-date thinking in the field of technical communication. Engineers and other technical personnel should avail themselves of this expertise whenever they pass reports through technical publication departments.

Technical Writing Means Business

An Important Process

Technical documentation can enhance the effectiveness of products when this documentation is produced as an integral part of product development—not as simply a second thought or a necessary evil.

Technical documentation is crucial to business efforts worldwide.

4

Know How You Fit into the Documentation Process

CONTENTS

Part of the Team

The Importance of Documentation

The documentation process is important to the production of products and services. The documentation process results in the production of proposals that attract business, manuals that describe operation of the company's products, specifications that describe parts and subsystems, reports that detail a company's internal and external functions, and various other documents.

Production of documents is often a team effort—and you are a vital part of that important team.

What You Will Learn

When you finish Chapter 4, you will

- Know the steps in the documentation process
- Know how you fit into the documentation process.

The Documentation Process

Where Do We Fit In?

Let's put our writing tasks in perspective. Where do our tasks fit into the documentation process? I want to discuss this so that you realize that *you are part of an important documentation team* and so that you can appreciate what others do in this process.

Understanding the Process

Each common task we perform can be broken down into specific steps or stages. With work-related processes, we need to identify the stages, understand them, and internalize them. By becoming familiar with these stages, we eliminate the need to "reinvent the wheel" each time we perform the tasks. Also, we can pass on the benefit of our experience to those who will perform these tasks in the future.

Step One: The Requirement

Every Document Has Requirements

Every document begins with a requirement to communicate an idea or a group of ideas to other human beings. The requirements become more detailed, depending on the information to be conveyed, the audience for the document, and the audience's needs. Requirements are discussed in Stage 1 (Chapter 5).

Step Two: The Writing Process

Elements of the Writing Task

Step two is the initial writing. The initial writing task includes gathering the appropriate material and organizing that material into the words, tables, and illustrations necessary to communicate the intended message. The original author might perform several iterations of the initial writing task before he/she is satisfied that the document has fulfilled all its requirements. The writing process is covered throughout this book.

Step Three: The Editing Process

The Editor's Responsibility

Enter the editor. Now it's time for a careful review of the manuscript. Does the document do the job that is desired and/or required? Does it do so clearly and without mechanical flaws such as spelling, grammar, and typographical errors? The editor is responsible for ensuring that the manuscript meets these minimal requirements.

A Fragmented Process

In a typical technical organization, the process of producing a technical document becomes more difficult to track at this stage. The author might submit his illustration requirements to the art department, and preparation of the artwork may be well advanced before the editor sees the manuscript for the first time. Likewise, complex tables may be submitted to word processing, composition, or whatever activity is appropriate. Thus, a number of individuals or groups may be working on pieces of the document simultaneously.

All this simultaneous work is necessary to meet a deadline. But it can be a significant source of stress to the editor. Does everything tie together? Is the nomenclature in the art and tables consistent with the nomenclature in the text? A company has a growing investment in each part of the document, and potential changes become more expensive every hour.

Quality Control

One or more quality control tests are normal when a manuscript is considered final but before final page makeup. In the cases of operating or maintenance manuals, quality control usually includes a test of all procedures in the manual to ensure that the procedures are correct and understandable. Someone other than the author of the document or the designer of the hardware/software should conduct the tests. One or more persons of authority may also choose to review the manuscript at this point.

Step Four: Page Makeup

The "Assembly Line"

When all parts of the document are correct and polished, we are ready for *step four: page makeup or composition.* The page makeup step can be compared to an automotive manufacturing production line. In the assembly line, we can visualize the various automobile subassemblies—hood, fenders, trunk, etc.—coming together to make the final product. In the page makeup "assembly line," the text must be prepared using the final sizes and styles of type. Each piece of art and each table must be carefully placed in relationship with the associated text. Art must be sized to fit. Material in the top and bottom margins of each page (running headers and footers) must be considered. If photographic artwork is to be included, mechanicals must be put into place.

Finishing Up

When all text, art, and tables have been laid out, the table of contents and other necessary indexes must be prepared. Upon conclusion of step four, the document can be called "camera-ready." In some cases, documents are reproduced by xerographic copying. In other instances, offset printing (using negatives) is appropriate. The negatives themselves might be a required delivery item (if the document is a military technical manual).

Quality Control

Since the camera-ready state represents the final appearance and content of the document, some quality control steps are normal at this point. Certainly some persons in authority within the organization will review and approve the document. Buying organizations also frequently require review at this point.

Step Five: Reproduction Tasks

The Finished Product

Step five encompasses all the varied reproduction tasks: making the negatives (if required), printing, collating, binding, and packaging for delivery.

Because of dramatic changes in the publishing industry, coupled with the differences in procedures among various organizations, we don't have time for a discussion of the many options involved in printing, binding, etc. Although the various reproduction alternatives are important for companies to consider, they are beyond the scope of MTW.

Playing To Win

Know Your Role

Documentation is a team effort, with each member of the team contributing to the success—or failure—of the product. The product speaks volumes about the team and the company. Each of us, no matter what our role in the production of documents, must be aware of the roles of others and be sensitive to their needs.

PART

3

The Technical
Writing Process

CONTENTS

TWP—The Nine-Point Plan

Processes—Part of Our Lives

Every day, we perform processes in our personal and professional lives. We learn, consciously or subconsciously, to perform each stage in these processes; therefore, we accomplish our tasks efficiently rather than haphazardly.

When we consciously know the stages in our processes, we can transfer that knowledge to others who can also benefit from our efficiency.

The Technical Writing Process

I want to pass on to you my understanding of the Technical Writing Process (TWP), a process that will help you write your documents more efficiently. This TWP has nine stages, which we will discuss in the following chapters.

Organization—The Technical Writing Process

Surveys of engineers show that engineers consider organizing documents the most difficult writing task. Engineers do not organize as effectively as they would like. Part of the problem is that they do not follow a process as they prepare, write, and revise their documents.

The stages of the Technical Writing Process are

- Analyze (requirements, audience, purpose)
- Gather information
- Brainstorm
- Categorize
- Sort
- Outline
- Design
- Write
- Revise.

The Technical Writer's Bookshelf

In working your way through the TWP, you may use the following books in conjunction with *Mastering Technical Writing*. These books will help answer a variety of questions that MTW does not address.

- Hodges, John C., et al. *Harbrace College Handbook.* San Diego: Harcourt Brace Jovanovich, Publishers, 1986.

This book helps you arbitrate knotty problems related to grammar. For example, is a particular indefinite pronoun singular or plural? Do you use an apostrophe for "employees cafeteria"? (Answer: Yes—"employees' cafeteria".)

- Brusaw, Charles T., et al. *Handbook of Technical Writing.* New York: St. Martin's Press, 1987.

This handbook describes the function of various technical documents—for example, progress reports, proposals, and manuals. It also discusses figurative language (e.g., metaphor) and rhetorical organization strategies (narrative, description).

- *United States Government Printing Office Style Manual.* Washington, D.C.: U.S. Government Printing Office, 1984.

If you write for the government, this style manual is invaluable. The *GPO Manual* contains accepted abbreviations, symbols, hyphenated words, titles, and the like.

- *The Chicago Manual of Style.* Chicago and London: The University of Chicago Press, 1982.

Commercial houses use *The Chicago Manual* as their "bible." It describes the front and back matter of manuscripts, the proper documentation style for bibliographies and references, and other matters.

- *The Random House Thesaurus.* New York: Random House, 1984.

Unlike *Roget's Thesaurus*, this book is organized alphabetically and contains a sentence illustrating the use of each word.

Why use a thesaurus? Not because you want to use more elevated words, but because you want to use the right word for a particular audience. A thesaurus allows you to travel up and down the scale of difficulty in your search for the right word.

- Flesch, Rudolf. *The Art of Readable Writing.* Rev. and enlarged ed. New York: Harper & Row, 1974.
- Flesch, Rudolf. *The ABC of Style: A Guide to Plain English.* New york: Harper & Row, 1980.
- Lanham, Richard A. *Revising Business Prose.* New York: Charles Scribner's Sons, 1981.

These books help communicators to develop a conversational, concise writing style.

> Stop reading now, and work through Exercise P3-1.

**EXERCISE P3-1
(Individual or Team)**

You can find the answers to the following problems by consulting the first five supplemental texts I have suggested.

1. How many kinds of abstracts are there?
2. You can identify the passive voice by determining whether the predicate contains a form of the verb *to be,* plus the past participle. Find definitions for passive voice, predicate, and past participle.
3. The audience you are writing for will not understand the word *opprobrious.* Find a synonym.
4. If you have two or more numbers appearing in a sentence, and one of the numbers is 10 or more, would you express the numbers in numerals or words?
5. Find a discussion of dangling modifiers. Then write a sentence containing a dangling modifier.
6. Should someone writing a document for the government hyphenate any of the words in the phrases *rust resistant covering* or *atomic energy power?*
7. In planning a journal article, what three questions should you ask yourself?

5 ·

Understand the Requirements, Audience, and Purpose of Documents

CONTENTS

Who, What, and Why

Remember Your Audience

Why do technical personnel, including engineers, have difficulty communicating with customers, other technical personnel, and nontechnical audiences?

Frequently, technical personnel overlook the audience and its requirements. This oversight results in an ineffective document.

What You Will Learn

This chapter represents Stage 1 of the TWP, analyzing the requirements, audience, and purpose of your document.

After working through this chapter, you will

1. Understand that you, as a communicator, need to know the requirements of your document. Customers will state certain requirements for their proposals, manuals, specifications, and the like. You *and* technical writers and editors need to know the general and specific requirements for each type of document.

2. Identify a representative group of sources that contain requirements for reports, proposals, manuals, and specifications.

3. Examine sections of these sources in order to know the kinds of requirements that will guide your writing.

4. Identify the audience for each of your documents.

5. List the relevant characteristics of your audience in order to more effectively appeal to that audience.

6. Determine the purposes for writing a document in order to more appropriately appeal to your audience.

7. Write purpose statements.

Attitude Check

Before you begin reading this chapter, review the following attitudes discussed in Chapter 1 of this manual:

- Writing is chiefly problem-solving (p. 15).
- Place important information at the front of the document (p. 21).
- Almost everyone should be prepared to write on the job (p. 22).
- We write for many audiences—and we must know them (p. 23).
- Begin to document as early as possible (p. 24).

Requirements

Why Understand the Requirements?

If it's not required, why do it? We are not pursuing this subject of communicating effectively for the sake of aesthetics or because it is a pet project. Technical writing style and organization are important because the government and other customers require us to communicate effectively.

Every Document Has Requirements

Every document begins with a requirement—to communicate an idea or a group of ideas to other human beings. For the fiction writer or essayist, this requirement may be only a drive in the author's head and heart. For the person writing a technical document, the requirement is likely to be more formal.

When organizations contract with each other to perform research, to design equipment, or to develop computer programs, *the buying organization typically requires simultaneous delivery of supporting documentation.* The larger the buying organization, the more likely it is that documentation requirements will be specified in considerable detail. The detailed requirements (specifications) will usually state the necessary content and organization and will sometimes specify voice, person, readability level, and other factors of immediate interest to the technical communicator. We call these *documented, or stated, requirements.* Other requirements, such as writing organized and concise text, are *implied requirements* which the customer may not stipulate, but exist nevertheless.

The Importance of Requirements

Why Meet the Requirements?

A completed research project has the potential to improve life for all mankind or, at the very least, to provide a foundation for additional progress. But the project is successful only when the methods and results are fully and clearly described so that others can use the new knowledge.

A new computer program may offer an easier way to perform a previously difficult task. It may promise time savings and efficiency to make people and organizations more effective. It may even make possible, calculations or analyses previously beyond the abilities of humans. But these wondrous things are possible only if the new software can be described clearly to others. Hence, the manuals that describe operation and maintenance of the software are critical, but the reports that detail the requirements and strategies for production of the software are also key pieces in the puzzle.

The Requirement to Communicate

Step one, then, is the requirement to communicate. The requirement may range from an intense desire to a detailed contractual obligation. We will assume that the information will be communicated by publishing, although the medium may be an oral presentation, film, video, or whatever. Once the requirement to publish is determined, the work must be planned, budgeted, organized, and scheduled. *Adequate planning includes an understanding of the objectives, content, and appropriate standards and specifications.*

Types of Requirements

Stated Requirements

Some requirements are *stated,* and others are *implied.* It may seem easy to follow the stated requirements of a contract, RFP, or military standard. However, people who prepare technical documents do not always follow stated requirements.

Example—CDRL Requirements

We may find stated requirements in a Contract Data Requirements List (CDRL). For example, we see the following reference in

"Attachment 1 to Contract F33657-88-C-0063, Mark XV IFF
System, Full Scale Development (FSD), Contract Data
Requirements List (CDRL)":

"SEQ NO	DID NO/TITLE/ SUBTITLE	SOW PARAGRAPH
1020	DI-S-4057	SOW Para 1030 .3 1"

This reference leads us to the Data Item Description (DID),
DI-S-4057, which states that "the report [one of the documents
specified in the CDRL] form, format, and content shall be in
accordance with MIL-STD-847."

Example—MIL-STD

MIL-STD-847, *Format Requirements for Technical and Scientific
Reports,* requires us to include certain elements in a report and in
a particular order:

> 5.1 *Elements of a report.* Although a report may not contain all of the
> following elements, those used will appear in the following order with
> the abstract appearing only on the Report Documentation Page, DD
> Form 1473:

> 5.1.1 Front matter.   Front cover (required)
> Report Documentation Page, DD Form 1473,
> (required)
> Summary

MIL-M-38784

Some standards impose stringent style requirements on writers.
MIL-M-38784, *Several Style and Format Requirements: Technical
Manuals*, page 38, requires the following:

> 4.4 *Validation of readability.* Narrative text shall be validated for
> conformance to readability standards specified in 3.3.3. Navy manuals
> prepared to meet the comprehension requirements of *DoD-STD-1685*
> shall be tested in accordance with the sampling criteria therein. If
> Overall Grade Level (OGL) (including tolerance) is exceeded, the
> manuscript shall be rewritten as required to meet specified Reading
> Grade Level (RGL). If sample Grade Level (GL) is exceeded, entire text
> surrounding each sample must be rewritten as required.

Readability Factors

To meet this stated requirement, we must evaluate readability factors (length of words and sentences, number of prepositional phrases, use of passive voice) as they apply to our audiences. We can do this by determining the readability index of selected passages in our documents.

Implied Requirements

Implied, or unstated, requirements also exist. Although MIL-STD-847 does not require authors to use readily understandable words or to write short sentences, the standard does say on, pages 5 and 6, that

> The prime purpose of a technical report is to disseminate the results of activity and to foster the exchange of information.

In order to "foster the exchange of information," we need to write clearly.

MIL-STD-490

Other military standards may state a requirement to write in a particular style. Page 7 of MIL-STD-490, *Specification Practices*, reads:

> 3.2.3 Language style. The paramount consideration in a specification is its technical essence, and this should be presented in language free of vague and ambiguous terms and using the simplest words and phrases. . . Consistency in terminology and organization of material will contribute to the specifications's clarity and usefulness. Sentences shall be as short and concise as possible. Punctuation should aid in reading . . . Well-planned word order requires a minimum of punctuation . . .

MIL-HDBK-2

MIL-HDBK-2, *Technical Writing Style Guide*, is a general reference and "does not supplant the official specifications nor any of the standard authorities," but does support the implied requirement that we communicate effectively. On page 3/1, the handbook states:

1. Arrange the parts of a sentence so that the meaning is clear on first reading.

2. Make sentences:
   - short
   - simple
   - concise

3. Rewrite sentences that are:
   - confusing
   - illogical
   - awkward
   - obscure

4. Break up long, complex, straggling sentences into several shorter ones.

Meeting the Requirements

Tailor the Document to the Requirements

Whether the requirements are *stated* or *implied*, we, as technical communicators, must use all of our written communication skills to satisfy those requirements. Tailor your products and documents. When a customer reaches for one of your documents, the *layout* of the document should invite the customer to read. Once involved in the document, the customer should be comfortable with its language and ideas.

Know the Audience

Do not limit your efforts to examining sources to discover customer requirements. Contact the audience and ask what information he or she would like to see in the document. Also, discover how the audience wants to see the information formatted. (We will discuss formatting more fully in Stage 7; see Chapter 11.)

Don't Change the Customer's Requirements

Also, once you know the requirements, adhere to them. Do not discover the customer's requirements and then say, "The customer wants A, B, and C, but I know better. The customer should have D, E, and F, and that's what I'll give them."

What can we do about the following attitudes?

- "The customer doesn't understand."
- "Let's give the customer our standard format."

The best way of doing things may not be the right way. *The customer's requirement defines the "best way."*

Sources for Requirements

Technical Report References

Consult the following references to ensure proper adherence to technical report requirements:

- *GPO Style Manual*
- *MIL-STD-847, Military Standard Format Requirements for Technical and Scientific Reports*
- *MIL-STD-38797, Writing and Editing Guide*
- *MIL-HDBK-63038-2, Technical Writing Style Guide*
- *Product Support/Data Management Style Guide.*

Additional References

Be familiar with the following standards governing the writing of other kinds of documents:

- *MIL-STD-490, Military Standard Specification Practices*
- *MIL-HDBK-63038-1A, Technical Manual Writing Handbook*

Know the Requirements

Know your customer's requirements, both the stated and implied requirements. You will find the stated requirements in contracts, military standards, and other such sources. If not stated somewhere, the major implied requirement is to write clearly.

A Useful Tool

You might ask your department to issue writing assignment sheets on which the person assigning the writing task can write detailed requirements. This way, both the person assigning the writing task and the writer are compelled to consider the requirements of the task before expending a significant effort.

> Stop reading now and work through Exercises 5-1 and 5-2 to learn more about working with requirements.

**EXERCISE 5-1
(Individual or Team)**

As an individual or a team, list the problems you encounter in discovering requirements for documents that you write.

Once you know the requirements, do you encounter problems acquiring resources to implement those requirements? If so, list those problems.

Take 10 minutes to accomplish Exercise 5-1.

**EXERCISE 5-2
(Individual)**

Writing Sample

Think of a project you have worked on or are currently working on. You have encountered a problem (technical, administrative, managerial) that you need to solve before you can complete the project.

Communicate this problem to the project manager or to someone else working on the project (your choice). The problem should be complex enough so that you can describe its various facets in a two-page report.

You will describe the problem in a two-page report, proposing a solution to the problem, if you like. Address the report, in a memorandum format, to a supervisor or colleague identifying the addressee by title.

Remember that the final draft of the report should be two pages long (single-spaced).

In order to generate this report, you will pass it through the stages of the Technical Writing Process (TWP), beginning with the Requirements/Audience/Purpose Stage and continuing through to the Revising Stage.

To begin the Writing Sample, list the stated and implied requirements of this two-page report. Include in this list, general style requirements and also particular style and management requirements found in to your area.

Take ten minutes to complete Exercise 5-2—listing the style requirements for your Writing Sample.

Your Audience

Remember Who's Reading

Often, the things that seem most obvious to us as authors are actually the least obvious in the documents we write. Only after we write the document and it fails to communicate do we problem-solve and ask, "Who is reading this document?"

Are you guilty of forgetting your audience when you write? If you are guilty, you have plenty of company. We all do it, and it's time to stop—now. We write for our audiences—not ourselves.

As technical communicators, we may write for a wide range of audiences—engineers, managers, military personnel, technicians, government auditors, and others.

Identify the Audience

Who Is Your Audience?

Just who is your audience? What are the audience's characteristics? These are key questions as you begin to prepare for your writing project.

Different audiences require different types of information. For a "lay" or low-level audience, you may need to use definitions and examples frequently to ensure that you are communicating your points. Also, you'll want to limit your use of jargon and acronyms. However, if you are writing for an expert audience, definitions and examples are unnecessary and may even be insulting. In addition, failure to use common jargon and acronyms may be a stumbling block to clear communication—besides possibly jeopardizing your credibility.

Questions About Your Audience

Before you begin writing any document, take time to ask some questions about your audience. Any or all of the following questions may apply:

- How much information does the audience need?
- What kind of information does the audience need?
- Does the audience need in-depth detail or a surface treatment?
- What is the audience's present knowledge base?

Depending on the audience's expertise (or lack of same), you may need to add definitions and examples while avoiding jargon.

- What is the audience's interest in the information?
- What is the audience's role in the organization?
- How long has the audience been in the organization?
- What will the audience do with the information?

If information will be used as a basis for another report, the information must be accurate. Consider using tables to quickly show interrelationships between data. Underscore significant conclusions and recommendations.

If information is to be used to repair equipment (as a manual), use as many graphics as possible. Also, don't use a perfect bind (a glued binding that does not allow a book to lie flat).

If information will be used on foils (visuals), provide some bulleted lists.

If information will be used in a section of a proposal, present the information according to the requirements for that particular proposal.

- What do you want the audience to do with the information?

This question relates to the primary and secondary purposes of the document. Straightforward purpose statements help; in addition, more subtle methods, such as the arrangement of your information, can also help accomplish your goals.

- What are the audience's sensitivities?
- What are the audience's biases?
- How much time does the audience have to read?

If time is short, summaries, bulleted lists, and tables are helpful.

Don't accept someone else's word for who your audience is and what your audience wants. Verify the audience profile yourself. Pick up the phone and ask people, or interview the audience in person, if possible.

Possible Technical Audiences—and Appropriate Techniques

Some typical technical audiences are listed below. For each audience listed, some "do's and dont's" for that audience are also included:

- Manager/Supervisor—Consider human and raw resources and use of time. Choose whether information should be in-depth or superficial. Establish the relevance of the information. Consider a problem-solution, general-to-specific, or most important-to-least important organizational pattern.
- Expert—Use specialized vocabulary and accepted methodology.
- User—Present descriptive procedures clearly. Use a simple vocabulary. Try to present only one idea per sentence.
- Technician—Use graphics frequently. Don't use a perfect binding.
- Technical expert—Place quantitative information first.
- Generic user—Consider using overviews, abstracts, and summaries to make reading easier. Add history and background information to ensure proper knowledge base. Include features/benefits (what's in it for me?). Make enjoyable through action titles, anecdotes, lighter tone, metaphors, etc. Consider using a general-to-specific or most important-to-least important organizational pattern.

- Multiple audience—Layer informations within sections. Break down sections into manageable chunks.
- Individuals forced to read documents—Motivate the audience with reasons for reading. Establish a "payoff."
- Younger audience—Use more contemporary language and a less formal approach.
- Older audience—Use more accepted phrasing and more formal approach.
- Internal audience—Appeal to working as a team to further company goals.

Learning About Your Audience

What Does the Audience Want?

Here's the scene: You're finishing an hour-long meeting. The moderator who called the meeting wraps up with

> Thanks for coming. I'm glad we got all of this hashed out. These are the action items: Tom, you take care of A, B, and C. And do so according to the procedure we discussed last week . . .

Tom accomplishes the three tasks in the prescribed manner and returns the following week to deliver a report on the results of his efforts. At the end of Tom's report, the moderator says

> That's well and good, Tom, but why didn't you do D and E, too? And, incidentally, you should have modified the procedure we discussed so that . . .

Often our audiences simply do not know exactly what they want. They have not thought out problems and solutions as fully as they might have. Sometimes, no cure exists for this problem. However, nail down your audience as much as possible. Sharpen your audience's thinking with questions, suggestions, whatever it takes so that you minimize your work and write the most tightly focused documents possible.

What Does the Audience Know?

Determine your audience's previous experience with your topic.

Are you repeating information the audience has already seen? If not, do you need to repeat some information for the sake of review or for some persuasive reason?

What Expertise Does the Audience Have?

What is the experience level of your audience? How long has your audience worked for its company? Has your audience taken an elementary, intermediate, or advanced course on this topic? Are the members of your audience beginners? Are they in the middle of the spectrum? Are they experts? Depending on where they are on the continuum of knowing, you should adjust the following:

- Vocabulary of your message
- Amount and kind of detail
- Amount and kind of exposition, or argument.

Don't Write in a Vacuum

When you write, think about your audience. Consider their needs, specifically:

- Their characteristics
- Their attitudes toward the topic
- Their problems and how those problems relate to your message
- The language they need to understand your message
- The most effective format for them
- How long they will sit still to understand your message.

The Importance of Benefits (What Does This Mean for Me?)

Throughout your document, tell your audience how they can benefit from reading your message. If you are writing a proposal, do not stop at listing features. Expand these features into benefits for your audience. For instance, if the customer requires positive stability (an aircraft's ability to maintain its course automatically without pilot guidance) in an ultralight aircraft, you *could* write the following:

> Our aircraft has positive stability and, therefore, meets the RFP requirement.

The above statement is accurate; however, you can influence your audience more with the following:

> Our aircraft has positive stability, thereby ensuring the safety of the pilot and aircraft—even when the pilot is unable to control the aircraft manually.

Don't just say something is good—tell your audience why it's good.

> Stop reading now and work through Exercise 5-3 to learn more about the audience for whom you write.

EXERCISE 5-3 (Individual)

List three audiences for whom you write and characteristics of those audiences.

Now, write a paragraph describing the audience for your Writing Sample.

Purpose

Different Documents, Different Purposes

Every type of document has a specific purpose or aim. For instance, progress reports communicate the status of projects. Proposals sell the company's products.

Writers should describe their purposes up front: "This report describes the progress I've made in developing *Mastering Technical Writing* (MTW). I began developing MTW four months ago. To date, I have completed the following modules: the Introduction, Chapters 5, 6, 7, and 10. I plan to complete the remaining modules according to this schedule . . ."

"Hidden" Purposes

Sometimes the purpose of a document may be hidden or less obvious. For example, the hidden purpose of a progress report may be to scrap a particular phase of a project. Similarly, the less obvious purpose of a proposal may be to expand the company's reputation in a particular product area. In some cases a company may submit a proposal, knowing that the proposal will fail, simply to satisfy the politics of a particular procurement situation.

Purpose—A Means to a Response

Underlying the purpose is a desired response we want from our audience. For example, in writing a proposal, we want the audience to respond favorably to our product or service. In writing a manual, we want the audience to understand the procedures covered and be able to use the equipment. Everything we say in our document should contribute to evoking the desired response in our audience.

Determine the Company's Purpose

If someone asked, "What is the purpose of a proposal," and you answered, "To sell the product," you would be half right. That is the apparent purpose. The less obvious purpose of a proposal is to sell the *company*, thereby selling the product. To achieve this purpose, the author must employ a number of company-selling techniques, among them a simple one: repeat the company's name judiciously throughout the proposal (instead of using the passive voice).

Determine the Audience's Purpose

Writers must consider their own purposes, their company's purposes, and their audience's purposes. With a proposal, the writer wants to sell the company; the audience wants to evaluate proposals accurately.

One audience, for instance, may weight the proposal sections in this way:

Category	Weight
Personnel	34%
Experience of Proposer	32%
Employee Relations	17%
Management Plans	9%
Corporate Commitment	8%

The audience's method of evaluating the proposal should drive the company's design of the document. In the case just presented, if you write a 100-page proposal, devote approximately 34 pages to personnel considerations, for instance.

Key Messages and Purpose

When you determine your document's purpose, don't forget to also formulate the key messages you want to convey to the audience. You may incorporate this step now, or later in the brainstorming stage.

What is the difference between purpose and key message? Your purpose might be to convince your audience to act; however, your key message might be that there is a resolvable problem in a particular area. When you write a proposal, your purpose might be to describe your approach, but your key message might be that your widget solves the customer's problem.

Develop a Purpose Statement

Writers can communicate the purposes of their documents by writing effective purpose statements. Make the purpose statement the first utterance in your document. Tell your audience right off what the document is about. When you state your purpose up front, the audience can more intelligently read your information.

Remember, you're not writing a novel in which you want to keep the suspense level high. You're writing a technical document, and your audience is searching, from the start, for information, for a framework on which to hang the information to come.

For example, if the first sentence in your document states that you are discussing defects in S-3A Power Supply Motherboard assemblies, then the audience can sweep through your report, gleaning related information and discarding extraneous material.

> Stop reading now and work through Exercises 5-4 and 5-5.

EXERCISE 5-4 (Individual)

Read through the following memo. Determine the memo's purpose, and then write a purpose statement for the memo.

TO: Jane Smith

COPY: Bob White

FROM: John Doe

SUBJECT: Resolution of Multiple Header/Insulator Thickness Phenomena:
Results of Feb. 6 Meeting and Additional Inquiries

On 2-4-87 a report was routed to the above individuals detailing information about numerous headers and insulators we will produce—reasons for numerous parts, production schedules and potential problems were reviewed. A meeting was held on 2-6-87 to review this information and evaluate problems and control mechanisms. Through this meeting and with additional inquiries, it was decided to control this situation by using different part numbers for each ceramic and retaining the same part number for the different header/insulator configurations at the first level of interchangeability—the array assembly. A list of the affected ceramic substrates, completed ceramics and array assemblies is on the next page.

As stated in the previous report, the current configuration is the standard (multiple piece base) 30 mils header with the standard 7 mils insulator. The supply of these parts will last

---

until approximately the end of April. At that time, production of the 7344 twenty-five mils standard headers will start (headers are the controlling factor, since insulator ceramics are plentiful and inexpensive). If the 25 mils standard headers supply becomes exhausted, and full production of the single piece base (SPB) headers has not begun, then production of standard 27 mils headers will start—this will be the first quarter of 1988.

Production of the SPB 25 mils headers for the qualification run will begin in early March. When the single piece base ECP receives approval and the qualification run is complete, production of 27 mils SPB headers will start.

SINGLE PIECE BASE CERAMICS:

	Thickness (mils)	Substrate P/N	Completed Ceramic P/N	Array Assy P/N
Insulator	10	539149-1	305956-1	305966
Header	27	306025-1	306026-1	
Insulator	12	539149-7	306020-1	305966
Header	25	305953-1	306018-1	

STANDARD CERAMICS:

	Thickness (mils)	Substrate P/N	Completed Ceramic P/N	Array Assy P/N
Insulator	7	539149-1	827078-1	872084
Header	30	803430-1	305996-1* 872083-1*	
Insulator	10	539149-1	306029-1	872084
Header	27	373414-1	306028-1	
Insulator	12	539149-7	306022-1	872084
Header	25	306021-1	306027-1	

The implications for the following areas are as follows:

CERAMIC FRONT END:

- Process with different AWOs and charge numbers for each ceramic.
- Upon completion of 30 mils standard headers, the following headers (25 mils) and insulators will be held until final assembly purges 30 mils headers.

- Distinct, color coded sheets will be applied to each set of ceramics: White for 30 mils standard headers and 7 mils insulators, green for standard 25 mils headers and 12 mils insulators, and yellow for the 25 mils SPB headers and 12 mils insulators—see attachment for example.

PRODUCTION CONTROL:

- Will not accept ceramics from front end without distinct, color coded paper designators.
- Assume responsibility for placing ceramics in appropriate separate places in final assembly C-lockers with color coded paper designators.
- 305996 is laser trimmed, while 872083 is photo-delineated.

FINAL ASSEMBLY:

- Responsible for assuring that ceramics are placed with proper AWOs. Final assembly AWOs will be color coded in the same manner as the ceramics.
- Process with different AWOs, but same charge numbers for each array assembly, that is, one charge number for standard and one for SPB array assemblies.

PROCESS CONTROL:

- For all areas, the primary focus for process control shall be the color coding of AWOs and ceramic supplies.
- Final assembly will have four other control methods to use. They are: (1) The automatic bonder will be out of focus in the event of a mismatch; (2) With a large mismatch, the bond may not hold; (3) Mismatches will not have the same look as proper matches and may be identified at inspection; (4) A micrometer is sensitive enough to identify even the smallest mismatch (2 mils) and should be used with questionable array assemblies.

IMPLEMENTATION:

- Documentation for three header/insulator pairs shall be addressed immediately. They are the standard 30+7 mils pair, the standard 25+12 mils pair, and the 25+12 mils

SPB pair. The 27+10 mils SPB pair will be set up with the advent of full SPB production. The standard 27+10 mils pair will be set up only if the SPB does not arrive before the standard 25+12 mils pair supply becomes exhausted.

The preceding control system will work only as well as everyone decides to make it work. It requires preventive rather than corrective actions, and thus could easily receive minimal attention—resulting in significant problems. It is imperative that people in the ceramic front end, quality control, production control, and final assembly are made aware of the implications and control of this situation through their respective supervisors, for it is only through this communication that we will succeed in preventing problems.

Your cooperation is appreciated.

Sincerely,

John Doe

EXERCISE 5-5 (Individual)

Write one to three sentences describing the purpose of your Writing Sample.

Narrow Your Aim

Define Audience, Requirements, and Purpose

Before you start writing, ask "Who will read this document?" and "What will the readers expect or require?" Unfortunately, these seem to be the last questions we ask. We concern ourselves first with pouring out the subject matter, without worrying about vocabulary, level of ideas, format, etc.

This mistake is not unusual. We rarely learn early in our educational life about audience. We think that only one audience exists—the teacher—and we carry this notion into our professional lives.

6 ·

Gather Information for the Document

CONTENTS

Read Better, Write Better

Reading—A Key Writing Skill

Reading is the first writing skill: Can you read (and understand) the requests that others submit and that demand a response from you? Can you quickly read the mountains of prose that you must sift through to gather information? Can you objectively read your own writing and others' and evaluate text for conciseness and coherence?

What Takes So Long?

Managers complain that too much time elapses between the time reports are assigned and the time they are finally produced. What pitfalls impede writers' progress in producing reports in a more timely manner?

A Few Simple Techniques

Writing documents need not be a long, drawn-out process. Reading dynamically—with speed and greater comprehension—can assist writers in finding important information to plug into their own documents.

What You Will Learn

This chapter presents Stage 2 of the TWP, gathering information.

After working through this chapter, you will learn how to read source documents and extract needed information more quickly.

Attitude Check

Before you begin reading this chapter, review the following attitudes discussed in Chapter 1 of this manual:

- Clear documentation takes time (p. 25).
- Writing clear documents takes great skill (p. 25).

Reading Techniques

Read Faster and Comprehend More

We read at an average speed of 250 words per minute; this is the speed at which we talk. When we first learn to read, we pronounce every word. Remember sitting in your first grade class and having the teacher say to you, "Okay, Johnny, please read the first paragraph from *Dick and Jane*"? You recited, haltingly, "See Dick run. See Jane run. See Dick and Jane run." You learned to see and pronounce every *single* word. In later grades, teachers asked you to read at your place, silently. You read silently, but you subvocalized; that is, you still pronounced each word, but not aloud.

We carry this reading method with us into our adult lives—unless we realize that the brain can process not hundreds of words per minute but thousands if we "remove our vocal chords" from the process. If we read with our eyes and our brain only, we can triple and quadruple our reading speed.

Learning to process words this new way takes work. It means adopting new attitudes and employing new techniques so that we can concentrate totally on reading.

Complete Concentration

Realize that reading, like any other serious activity, takes total concentration. If you're playing tennis *and* daydreaming, soon tennis balls will be bouncing off your head.

A Scenario—How We Lose Concentration

Follow this scenario for a moment: You sit down in a comfortable chair in your cubicle, put your feet up, and open a chemistry text. Soon, you find yourself reading about a combination of substances that has resulted in a green compound. Your subconscious pauses and says, "Green. Hmm. A green meadow. A picnic basket on the green meadow. A friend. Cold chicken. Beer. Champagne. A sunny day." And you drift off to a much better world. You return from your trip 10 minutes later and discover that you have "read" 15 pages. (You were conscious enough to turn pages during your reverie!) Time to get up and take a break from the world of chemistry. We fool ourselves into thinking that we have "read" when, in fact, we have sleepwalked.

We should read when we are refreshed, at a time of day when our energy level is high. We should sit at a chair that supports us, and we should dismiss the rest of the world for this period of time.

Pacing Yourself Promotes Concentration

Pace yourself through your reading. Some reading experts recommend *pacing with the hand*—guiding the hand down the page in some patterned motion, forcing the eyes to read more quickly than they are used to. Simply underlining each line of text with the hand from left to right produces good results. Pacing promotes concentration and increases speed. Pacing breaks the habit of dwelling on particular words. I have found myself, for no good reason, savoring structure words like *moreover, further, is,* and *to* or lingering over linguistically interesting content words whose meanings I perceive instantly—instead of concentrating on reading and understanding as much as I can.

Pacing drills develop necessary "physical," eye-hand reading skills.

Reading skills resemble the skills we develop when we learn a sport. We don't simply step onto a basketball court and know how to dribble, pass, and shoot. Coaches drill us, work us hard on fundamentals. In time, we develop the physical skills needed to play the game. The same is true of reading. Teachers can drill us on fundamentals so that we develop the necessary reading skills. And, as in sport, we can also practice our skills on our own.

Perceiving Ideas

Consider the way we perceive, or "read," the world around us. We walk into a meadow and we look. We do not say, "There is the sky. There is a tree. I see another tree. I see birds in a tree. I see the grass. And there is a cow." We don't read the details of the picture individually; we see the whole picture instantly. We do not need to read individual words to see the whole idea individual words represent.

Consider also that we need not pronounce individual words in their logical sequence in order to grasp whole meaning. If someone writes, "The ball John kicked," you read that to mean "John kicked the ball." A mechanism in your consciousness assembles logical meaning even when writers fail to represent meaning logically.

Structure Words Vs. Content Words

Words generally fall into two categories: content words and structure words. Content words are those that carry the meaning of the sentence; structure words are those that tie the sentence together but carry no meaning. Of the 600,000 words in *Webster's International Dictionary*, 70 percent are content words and 30 percent are structure words. But the structure words are used so frequently that they compose 70 percent of our written and spoken language. Still our minds sift through the mass of words, discarding the meaningless structure words and accepting the content words. The mass of content words shapes the meaning of what we read.

Practicing Your New Reading Methods

Let your eyes fall on the following passage. Do not read each word. Read for content. Glance at the passage in the same way that you would glance at a view outside your window. The idea is to preview the passage—rapidly organize and assess it. The passage has an overabundance of structure words; additionally, some structure and content words are presented in illogical patterns. Notice how the mass of these content words, no matter what order you read them in, "add up" to one whole idea:

ASSET GIMBAL DESCRIPTION

The ASSET gimbal system (figure 2) designed and built by the Northrup Corp. as a testbed for alternate night/day sight and laser designs is a four gimbal system. The two outer gimbals are used as slaves to the inner gimbals and are used in an azimuth/elevation configuration. The two inner gimbals are used for inertial stabilization and are in an elevation/cross-elevation configuration. The designation of these gimbals will be outer AZ, outer EL, inner EL, and inner X-EL. The outer EL gimbal contains the windshroud to protect the inner gimbals from aerodynamic disturbances. The inner X-EL gimbal, of course, contains the FLIR, Day TV, and LASER.

The gimbal's system control processor and the Servo Electronics Unit are located in the electronics bay (figure 3) of the helicopter just behind the pilot seats. The control processor does the initial BIT for the system and allows the operator to control the operation modes of the system. The servo electronics unit contains the servo compensation boards for both rate and position loops and power supplies. The other servo components such as the gyros, gyro preamp boards, and the motor drive amplifier boards are located on the gimbal.

The stabilization rate loops are type 2 designs using the rate-integrating gyro in a rate integrating mode. The compensation network is two lead-lag filters with a second order low pass. There are notch filters at the gyro bearing retainer frequency and gyro spin frequency to reduce power consumption in the motor power supply, and two adjustable notches for structural resonances.

Stabilization servo/gimbal parameters are listed in Table 1 as measured, estimated by measurement/analysis, and supplemented by the Northrup servo report.

How Did You Do?

What whole idea did you perceive? In order for these new methods to work, we need to gain confidence in our native ability to "read information" at a glance.

As you grasp whole ideas and see the whole picture, ask questions as you read. Make connections among facts. This strategy demands that you read actively, that you hunt for meaning. The questions you ask, such as the five W's (Who? What? When? Where? Why?), provide a kind of flypaper for the meaning contained in your reading. The questions you ask form a matrix in which you may post memorable details.

Stop reading now and work through Exercise 6-1.

**EXERCISE 6-1
(Individual)**

You will need a timing device for this exercise.

The purpose of this exercise is to increase your reading speed and comprehension by breaking down old attitudes and developing eye-hand coordination. As you read, you will concentrate totally on your reading task.

First, read the following nine-page selection for one minute, as you ordinarily would read. Do not speed up your usual rate. Mark the place where you left off after reading for the one minute. When you finish reading for one minute, record the total number of words you read. You may do this by counting the number of words in the first three lines of the selection and dividing by three to find an average per line. Then multiply that figure by the number of lines on a full page of the selection for the total number of words per minute. Record the words per minute (WPM) figure.

Now add one page to your original reading. Go back to the beginning of the selection and read what you originally read, plus the added page—still within the one-minute time limit. (You'll ask yourself how you can read an additional page within the one-minute period. Remember you've already read much of this information one time before.) This time, though, pass the fingertips of your hand under each line that you read. Let your hand pace you through your reading. Read for good comprehension, but push yourself to read to your new mark.

Repeat this procedure three more times, adding two more pages to the original reading the first time, four pages the second time, and finally eight pages the third time. In each case, make your mark . . . even if you must sacrifice comprehension.

When you have finished reading for the fifth time, find a new part of the selection—one that you have not read before. Now, read that new section for one minute, using your hand as a pacer. Mark the place where you finish.

How many words did you read this sixth time? Did you double your reading speed? Come close to doubling?

SECTION V
HANDBOOK DEVELOPMENT

5-1.   <u>INTRODUCTION.</u>

5-2.   The primary responsibility of the technical writer is to fulfill the contractual requirements for technical manuals. This includes meeting all specification requirements, providing accurate and adequate coverage for the equipment involved to the specified level of maintenance, delivering manuals on schedule, and doing all this within the established budget. This section deals with the tasks involved in fulfilling this responsibility and the order in which these tasks should be performed.

5-3.   <u>PLAN.</u>

5-4.   The first step in almost any endeavor is planning. Without planning the work tends to be disorganized leading to false starts and wasted effort. Therefore, PLAN YOUR WORK. First, learn all aspects of the job. To establish a manuscript plan, figure 5-1, the following must be defined or developed:

> Requirements
> Schedule
> Budget
> Outline

5-5.   REQUIREMENTS. Prior to devising a schedule, it is necessary to define the requirements for the types of manuals and the maintenance philosophy. This type of information is used in the quoting phase as well, but a thorough review is required at this point to ensure adequate coverage within the technical manuals. The following paragraphs provide guidelines for determining the types of manuals and the maintenance philosophy.

5-6.   Types of Manuals. The contract will contain documents that describe the types of manuals required and the specifications that control content and format. Obtain copies of applicable specifications and start the skeleton of the preliminary outline based on the specifications. Depending upon the customer, this skeleton may be only a list of the required sections or it may be a fairly detailed list of suggested paragraph heads. When this task is finished, a set of documents should be available that not only identifies the types of manuals required, but will also form the nucleus of the more detailed outlines to follow. Section III provides details of the outline development.

5-7. Maintenance Philosophy. Maintainability will normally develop the maintenance philosophy if it is not established by contract. Whether the maintenance philosophy is established by contract or not, the maintainability engineer is an excellent source of information on what the customer authorizes at the various levels of maintenance. Later in the program, a provisioning conference with the customer will establish Source, Maintenance, and Recoverability (SM&R) codes which will identify exactly what is repairable, what is replaceable, and at what level of maintenance this repair or replacement can be accomplished.

5-8. SCHEDULE. The same contract documents that specify the types of manuals required specify the delivery date. Usually technical manual delivery requirements are specified relative to hardware deliveries. This means that it will be necessary to estimate the milestones that make up the performance/delivery schedule. This is called scheduling and will be covered in some detail later in this section.

5-9. BUDGET. The budget, the amount of money available for the job, is established by negotiation with the program manager. Obtain the project file and review the quotation history. Determine how the job was evaluated and how much was orginally quoted. Study the contract noting any scope of effort changes that might affect the cost. Use all the foregoing information to prepare a suggested budget, complete the justification for any differences between the budget and the quote that went to the customer, to negotiate the final budget with the program manager.

5-10.   OUTLINE. The usual contract calls for the design and development of hardware, and, if a computer is part of the hardware, software may also be required. Contact engineering to determine as much as possible about the hardware, its function, configuration, and how it works. If documentation such as schematics, equipment specifications, and test procedures is available, obtain copies for reference. The more that is known about the hardware/software when starting the scheduling and outlining the manuals, the more accurate the schedules and outlines will be. Refer to Section III for outline development.

5-11.   SUMMARY. After all this information is gathered, it is time to make some plans. It is possible to identify the problem areas, if any, and start making plans to solve or avoid the problems before they become emergencies. For example, if the budget is inadequate, find justification for a change-in-scope or identify some shortcut that will enable the job to be done within the budget. If the schedule is such that more people are required, this must be brought to the attention of the supervisor while there is still time to do something about it. The sooner problems are recognized and action is taken to solve them, the better the chances for successfully completing the job.

5-12.   SCHEDULE.

5-13.   The schedule is a record of the milestones that must be completed to accomplish the task. Refer to figures 5-2 and 5-3 for the tasks and flow of a job from manuscript development through end item development. These illustrations represent a typical flow for the development of a technical manual. Figure 5-4 is a sample schedule showing the milestones on a time line to indicate when each milestone must be completed. Properly updated, the schedule can become a record of performance when the job is finished. In developing the schedule, use all available information. The following is a representative list of milestones in a typical schedule.

Publications Guidance Conference (Pubs Guidance Conference)
Outline
Illustrations
In-Process Review (IPR)
Manuscript
Engineeering Review
Validation
Preliminary Technical Orders (PTO) Production
PTO Delivery
Verification
Final Production
Prepublication Review (Pre-pubs Review)
Negatives

The foregoing list does not include all milestones for every situation, nor are all the milestones listed required in all cases. This list and the sample schedule of figure 5-4 are intended to be typical examples only. Usually the schedule will be developed by starting with the hardware delivery schedule which establishes PTO delivery. For this reason, the milestones discussion will be in reverse order, starting with PTO delivery. The discussion will conclude with VERIFICATION, FINAL PRODUCTION, PRE-PUBS REVIEW, and NEGATIVES.

5-14.   PTO DELIVERY. This is the key milestone in setting up the schedule. It is a contractual date that must be met, and usually it is tied to the hardware delivery. Since PTOs usually infer that validation has taken place, it must be remembered that all the hardware (prime and support equipment) must be available for validation. Once the PTO delivery milestone is set, the other milestones can be estimated.

5-15.   PTO PRODUCTION. These milestones mark the time frame that the manuscript is in production. The Technical Publications group has several options for accomplishing large jobs on a short schedule. However, they also serve a lot of customers; therefore, scheduling problems and priorities may impact the time required for each job.

5-16.   VALIDATION. Validation is the process by which the contractor tests a manuscript for technical accuracy at Texas Instruments or at the contractor's facility. It entails the actual performance of operating and maintenance procedures. The starting and completion milestones for validation are usually very tight when it comes to schedule. Sometimes hardware is tied up for qualification testing or training. If the equipment is to be drop-shipped, the date should be the start date. Drop-shipped hardware is hardware that has been sold to the customer but is left at Texas Instruments for the purpose of training or validation. If validation is to be done prior to the hardware delivery date, engineering should be consulted to determine a start date. The length of time required for validation depends upon the complexity of the hardware, available time on the hardware, and the maintenance philosophy. The completion date will depend upon the starting date and the time involved for validation. Normally two to four weeks are required to incorporate validation comments into the manuscript.

5-17.   ENGINEERING REVIEW. This review should be scheduled when a section/chapter of the manuscript is complete. It is not necessary to wait until the entire manuscript is complete to schedule a review. The main object is to permit engineeering to review the material as soon as possible to correct errors and to rectify writer misconceptions. The more comprehensive the engineering review, the less problems can arise at validation.

5-18.   MANUSCRIPT. The completion of these milestones is a prerequisite for validation. Manuscript-complete marks the assembly of draft text and tabular material with draft or final illustrations into a relatively complete manual. Before completing the manuscript, invite the customer to witness validation, and make necessary arrangements for facilities, hardware, and test equipment.

5-19. IN-PROCESS REVIEW. In-process reviews (IPR) are held at interim points in manuscript development to permit Texas Instruments and the customer to jointly review data, produced to that point, for content and format. The IPRs are a matter of customer/Texas Instruments' choice and may be scheduled at any point during manuscript preparation. Schedule IPRs from information in the contract or from the customer. Otherwise, wait until after the publications guidance conference to schedule IPRs.

5-20. ILLUSTRATION START. These milestones mark the time frame for writer input of sketches to the illustrating department. The start milestone should be placed as early in the schedule as possible. Start developing illustrations to support the text as soon as they are identified.

5-21. OUTLINE. If the contract requires the delivery of an outline, delivery will usually be specified as being required 30 to 60 days after start of technical manual effort. For this purpose, start of technical manual effort is usually interpreted to mean the publications guidance conference. If valid engineering data is available, work on the manuscript and the outline can be done concurrently. If the data is available, lead-in sentences, tables of leading particulars, power requirements, etc. as well as figure titles, can be included in the outline. However, if the design is in the early stages, the actual start of manuscript development should be postponed until firm information is available. Starting manuscript development too soon will result in wasted time and budget. On the other hand, starting too late will jeopardize the remainder of the schedule.

5-22. PUBLICATIONS GUIDANCE CONFERENCE. The pubs guidance conference is the first event of the handbook development process. This is where the writer and the customer get together to discuss the program. The customer will clarify the requirements in terms of what is required and what reviews to schedule. Ask questions and discuss Texas Instruments interpretation of the requirements. The minutes will serve as a guide during the development of the handbook. If the customer does not schedule the conference soon after contract award, and a requirement exists, prepare a letter requesting that a conference be scheduled and forward it through the program manager and the contract administrator. Conference requirements include, but are not limited to, the following: unfamiliar specifications, format, content, unique end item, or readability level.

5-23.   VERIFICATION. Verification is the process by which the Preliminary Technical Order (PTO) is tested and proven by the customer. It consists of actual performance on the equipment of procedures in the PTO by customer personnel. The writer's obligation at verification is to provide technical assistance when requested. The actual schedule for performance of verification is at a time and location agreed to between Texas Instruments and the customer after the PTO has been delivered. For scheduling purposes, allow 60 days after PTO delivery to permit customer review and evaluation prior to verification.

5-24.   PREPUBLICATION REVIEW. This review gives the customer an opportunity to ensure the verification comments have been incorporated and examine the reproducible copy before page negatives are prepared. The customer often specifies a 30-day time frame between verification and prepublication review. As a practical matter, take issue with the 30-day requirement and suggest that 45 or 60 days would be a more realistic schedule. Work this problem through the contract administrator. The time required for the review can be estimated by dividing the total number of pages by 300. The result will be an approximation of the number of days required to complete the review.

5-25.   NEGATIVES. These milestones represent the time required to prepare and check the negatives. The time frame depends upon the size of the job. Allow one day to reassemble the final repro package and input it into reproduction. The time to prepare the negatives will have to be extracted from the quote. Allow a maximum of one day per 300 negatives for the data manager check cycle. Notify the data manager when the job for negatives is input to production so that paperwork can be prepared for delivery of the negatives.

5-26   METHODS.

5-27.   The following paragraphs describe the various methods used in generating technical manuals. Organization helps prepare the writer to do the job efficiently and in an orderly manner. The Generation of Text and Tabular Pages and the Generation of Illustrations paragraphs are provided to help the writer determine what needs to be generated, where the information may be found, and some of the various ways to do the job.

5-28.   ORGANIZATION. The writer has a much better chance of producing an effective manual if all the requirements are clearly organized and understood before the actual writing begins. An organized effort makes the writer's job of putting the words on paper much easier. The writer needs to know and understand the contract requirements, maintenance philosophy, and specification requirements. Any doubts or questions concerning these requirements should be resolved before progressing further in developing the manuals. The Pubs Guidance Conference is a good way to solve these problems. If the contract calls for an outline to be delivered, it is required at the beginning of the program. Since this is usually the first contractual deliverable item, it should be started first. Section III explains how to develop outlines.

If an outline is not required by contract, it is still best to generate one as the outline will show the organization of the manual.

5-29.   GENERATION OF TEXT AND TABULAR PAGES. Before generating any text or tabular pages the writer should have the outline generated. Figure 5-5 is a sample topical outline showing the usual order of topics. The specific technical manual outline will identify Chapter/Section number and title as well as Paragraph number and title, and will be tailored to the specifications called out in the contract. The manual should not necessarily be generated in the order the outline is laid out. Certain portions of the manual should be written before other portions because of the learning curve involved. For example, write the theory of operation, and controls and indicators before attempting testing or troubleshooting, and write testing before attempting troubleshooting. Try to write portions of the manual first that will enable later portions to be written more efficiently because of the knowledge learned in the previous portion. The following paragraphs relate to the outline in figure 5-5 and explain what the paragraph should contain and where the information may be found.

5-30.   Introduction. This paragraph introduces the manual. The information is usually boilerplate material from a similar manual.

5-31.   Scope and Arrangement. This paragraph explains how the manual is organized. It explains the contents of the different sections, chapters, or work packages. This information can be obtained from the detailed specification or the outline.

5-32.   Related Publications. This paragraph will reference other technical manuals related to the maintenance of the equipment. This usually includes the related prime equipment and/or test equipment manuals.

5-33.   Description. This primary sidehead introduces the physical, electrical, and functional descriptions of the equipment.

5-34.   Physical Description. This secondary sidehead provides a physical description of the equipment (length, height, depth, weight, cooling requirements, etc.). This information may be available in the equipment specification or obtained from drawings or engineering.

5-35.   Electrical Description. This secondary sidehead provides an electrical description of the equipment (power requirements, major input and output signals, etc.)

NOTE

In some detail specifications, the physical and electrical descriptions are called leading particulars and will be required to be in tabular format.

5-36.   Functional Description. This secondary sidehead usually contains several paragraphs describing what the equipment does functionally and refers to an overall block diagram for better understanding. Each paragraph should cover a major function of the equipment. A block diagram may be available in the equipment specification, or engineering may have already developed one.

5-37.   Preparation for Use and Reshipment. This primary sidehead usually introduces two secondary sideheads; unpacking and packing.

5-38.   Unpacking. This secondary sidehead tells how to unpack the equipment upon receipt. Information concerning how the equipment is packed for shipment will usually be available from engineering or the packing and shipping department. This information can be used for developing unpacking procedures. Unpacking should include procedural steps necessary to make the equipment ready for use.

5-39.   Packing. This secondary sidehead tells how to pack the equipment in preparation for shipment. These procedures are usually a reversal of the unpacking procedural steps.

5-40.   Principles of Operation. This primary sidehead usually introduces several paragraphs which provide functional and/or detailed theory of how the equipment and its subassemblies operate. Depending upon the maintenance philosophy, it may refer to detailed block diagrams or schematic diagrams. This information is an analysis of detailed block diagrams or schematics and usually has to be generated for the manuals. The schedule, availability of engineering assistance, maintenance philosophy, skills of the writer, etc., will be factors which determine who will generate the principles of operation. The writer should always try to develop as much of the manual as possible while staying within the budget and schedule guidelines.

5-41.　Testing and Troubleshooting. This primary sidehead introduces the operational checkout and troubleshooting. These are usually procedural steps, logic-type diagrams, or tables. Whichever method is used, the testing and troubleshooting must be tied to each other in some manner. These procedures must be generated from the theory of operation, acceptance test procedures, knowledge of the test equipment, wiring lists, and the schematic diagrams.

5-42.　Alignment or Calibration. This primary sidehead introduces the alignment procedures for the prime equipment or the calibration procedures for the test equipment. The alignment or calibration procedures are usually generated after testing because of the learning curve. The alignment and calibration procedures are usually procedural steps. A source of information is the calibration measurement requirements summary (CMRS).

5-43.　Cleaning. This primary sidehead introduces the proper materials and procedures used to clean the equipment. This is usually boilerplate material.

5-44.　Inspection. This primary sidehead usually introduces the visual inspection requirements. This is usually boilerplate material.

5-45.　Disassembly and Assembly. This primary sidehead usually introduces two secondary sideheads, disassembly and assembly. These are usually procedural steps that describe how to disassemble and assemble the equipment. Sometimes disassembly and assembly will be covered by two primary sideheads.

5-46.   Tables. Tables are often the most effective means of presenting information. Information that is listed, compared, ordered, or a function of other conditions naturally lends itself to tabular presentation. A well-thought-out table is a valuable information resource. The writer must organize tables so that the information contained is easily perceived. Accurate, descriptive titles are important for rapid identification of the purpose of the table. A table should always be located as close as possible to the text that references it.

5-47.   Headings. Technical manuals are usually divided into sections, chapters, or work packages. These main divisions are usually divided further into sideheads. The specifications usually clearly state the designation of sideheads and their use.

5-48.   Warnings, Cautions, and Notes. With few exceptions, it is standard practice to highlight procedures that if incorrectly performed could produce adverse consequences to the equipment or personnel. These procedures are usually preceded by WARNINGS, CAUTIONS, or NOTES that alert the manual user to a critical step. Examples are shown in figure 5-6.

5-49.   Checklists. Checklists are a specific sort of tabular material. They are abbreviated procedures and inspection steps. Checklists are used for quickly locating and recording quality assurance procedures that are critical steps.

5-50.   Front Matter. Front matter generally consists of the cover, title page, and numerical index. It can also include a list of tables and list of illustrations. The front matter is usually generated last. The particulars for the preparation of front matter are detailed in the applicable specifications for the manual.

Picking Up the Pace

Reading Dynamically Impacts the TWP

Learn to read more quickly and to comprehend more of what you read. Then notice how much more quickly you can move through the stages of the TWP.

7 ·

Brainstorm the Information

CONTENTS

Brainstorm Your Ideas

Order Out of Chaos

The first step in organizing a document is an exercise in *disorganization* called brainstorming, or free-associating the ideas connected with the document you will write.

A brainstorming session may result in notes that look something like this:

BLOCK MOVES USING WORDSTAR

Use KB and KK
Moving sentences
Moving paragraphs
Moving blocks from one file to another
How to hide markers
How to copy blocks from one place to another
Does WordStar accomplish block moves more efficiently than other wp packages?
How often does the writer use the block commands?

As you can see, the ideas in these notes do not flow in any logical fashion. When you brainstorm, you jot down ideas as they occur to you without monitoring them. This allows an unrestricted outpouring of information. Later, you revise this outpouring of data.

What You Will Learn

This chapter presents Stage 3 of the TWP, brainstorming the information.

When you complete this chapter, you will understand the usefulness of brainstorming.

Attitude Check

Before you begin reading this chapter, review the following attitude discussed in Chapter 1 of this manual:

- Show your ignorance—ignorance is required (p. 21).

How to Brainstorm

Let Yourself Go

Brainstorming is simply a way to gather ideas about your document and put the ideas on paper—with no regard to their ultimate place in your document. This step allows you to consider all facets of your document, without the constraints of organization.

Brainstorming should not produce tension. No one will see the thoughts and ideas you write down. Brainstorming is simply a preliminary step conducted before you begin to produce your document. When you brainstorm, let your consciousness range over the spectrum of information related to your document, and then jot down the thoughts you develop.

A Few Rules for Brainstorming

The following rules pertain to brainstorming:

1. Gather as much available information as possible. Fill yourself up before beginning the session. Be ready to overflow onto the page.
2. Don't restrict yourself to the format or grammar (including parallel structure) of the ideas.
3. Accept words, phrases, or complete thoughts. The brainstorming session is not an outline.
4. Don't monitor the order of your thoughts. Place them on the page as they occur to you.
5. Once the ideas are down, don't analyze or evaluate them. You will do this in later stages.

> Stop reading now and work through Exercises 7-1 and 7-2 to see more about how brainstorming works.

**EXERCISE 7-1
(Individual)**

When we write, what else are we doing?

We're thinking ahead, we're revising, we're evaluating. we're problem-solving. These steps are good in their proper place—but don't do them when you're brainstorming. Don't interrupt the flow of information. You are capturing information when you brainstorm. Save the evaluating and revising for later stages of the TWP.

Now, brainstorm the material you will need in order to write your two-page Writing Sample.

**EXERCISE 7-2
(Team)**

Brainstorm in teams so that you can unearth more information for your document.

Choose two or three teammates. Take five to seven minutes to brainstorm ideas for each team member's document. Don't evaluate the inputs from team members; remember, evaluation of brainstorming material comes later.

Free-Form Comes First

A Valuable Approach

Brainstorming is a valuable, possibly playful approach to discovering the breadth of information you may use in a document. Do not bypass this important step and attempt to logically organize from the start—you may inadvertently omit important information.

8 ·

Categorize the Information

CONTENTS

How Can You Categorize?

Developing Your Ideas

Throughout the week, you write yourself notes about the errands you will run on the weekend. When the weekend comes, you collect the notes with the following directions:

- Buy carrots
- Buy shoelaces
- Buy potatoes
- Buy wine
- Buy lettuce
- Buy beer
- Buy Lean Cuisine frozen meals
- Have shoes fixed
- Take Andrew to his basketball game
- Fill prescription for dog's skin condition
- Take Sara to her ballet lesson
- Ice cream.

Categorizing Your Ideas

You take all of the separate notes and categorize them according to a scheme:

Supermarket   Kids' Activities   Drugstore   Liquor Store

So, from chaos comes order. In the same fashion, with our documents, from chaos (brainstorming) comes order (categorizing). In the categorizing stage, you begin to impose order on your thoughts by choosing appropriate headings for the information you have brainstormed.

What You Will Learn

This chapter presents Stage 4 of the TWP, categorizing information.

After completing this chapter, you will

- Write headings for the information you discovered in the brainstorming stage.
- Arrange information under appropriate headings.

Attitude Check

Before you begin reading this chapter, review the following attitudes discussed in Chapter 1 of this manual:

- Organize information as tightly as possible (p. 20).
- Use action titles (p. 20).

Classifying Information

Organize Information After You Brainstorm

After your brainstorming session, the next step in the TWP is to categorize (label) all of the information from your brainstorming. You will select some of the information, delete some, and merge other information.

Headings

In order to label your ideas, you need headings and subheadings. Some examples of headings and subheadings are

- Introduction
- Body
- Conclusion
- Purpose
- Definition
- Appendix
- Overview.

Use Action Titles

While you categorize (classify), consider your headings and subheadings (labels). Try to improve them whenever possible. Consider converting headings and subheadings to *action titles.*

Look at the headings presented above—Introduction, Body, Conclusion, etc. These one-word headings say little about the content of the sections other than to mark the position of the section within the document. For instance, audiences know that a preface appears before the table of contents and tells something about the author's approach to his subject. Consider rephrasing the heading "Preface" in more specific terms, like "Computer Commands Everyone Can Understand."

Some headings, such as "Appendix," are a red flag to audiences, inviting them to ignore whatever follows. If we want to appeal to our audiences, we must work to capture their attention. Instead of "Appendix," use a more active title such as "Complete Research Information" or "Detailed Data That Supports Our Findings." Either of these titles tell the audience that the section contains additional information that they may want to review.

Tip off your audience with action titles. Lead the audience along the path of your message as directly as possible. Action titles serve as mini-abstracts for your audience, letting them know whether they need to read a particular section.

Examples of Action Titles

Review the following action titles to determine how you can improve your documents.

- Four Steps Necessary to Move Text
- Three Characteristics of the Passive Voice
- XYZ Corporation Proposes MWIR Band
- XYZ Corporation and the U.S. Navy: Partners in Missile Development
- Rand and Roberts, Inc. Offers Two Solutions to the Air Force's Problem.

If You Have Problems Creating Action Titles

Consider using any or all of the following elements:

- Your company's name
- The customer's name
- Problems
- Solutions
- Verbs to denote action
- Independent clauses
- Numbers.

Heading Styles Help You Organize

"Set" action titles according to levels. For example, you could organize headings as follows:

- First level—Flush left, all capitals
- Second level—Flush left, initial capitals, underlined

- Third level—Flush left, initial capitals
- Fourth level—At the beginning of a paragraph (indented), initial capitals, underlined, followed by a period, then two spaces and text.

EXAMPLE

ENGINEERS AT FORD DISCUSS NEW ENGINES

Ford engineers have developed a unique internal combustion engine which burns a mixture of gasoline and alcohol. The new engine contains features not found in previous models of the internal combustion engine.

Features of the New Gasahol Engine

The new engine differs, primarily from former engines, in that it will burn a combination of fuels. Second, the new engine does not employ pistons as its driving force. Rather, ... The engineers have developed three modifications of this new internal combustion engine.

Eagle I Develops 375 Horsepower

> *The First Modification.* The first modification involves...

> Stop reading now and work through Exercise 8-1 to practice classifying information you have brainstormed.

EXERCISE 8-1 (Individual)

On a separate piece of paper, create relevant headings for your brainstorming session and, in a rough way, arrange bites of information under appropriate action titles.

When you finish the exercise, read the related discussion on the following pages.

Prototypes

A Way to Categorize

When you categorize your information, you create a skeleton of action titles/headings for the information in your document. This emerging skeleton gives rise to a prototype. For instance, we remember a certain base representation, of "car." We represent car with roof; body, including fenders; lights; engine; transmission; wheels; axles; and tires. We also hold corrections to the prototype in memory. We represent corrections with the details of a specific car—like a DeLorean with its gull-wing doors, stainless steel body, and teardrop shape. In terms of where this information is held in memory, we place the prototype close to the top of memory because we access the representation regularly. We place the corrections below the top because we access that information less frequently. Recognizing the prototype, plus corrections, of a document helps you to classify the information in your document.

Tables—Another Way to Categorize

Tabular or Grid Format

In the Categorize stage, consider placing information into a table, once you identify your prototype. Your information may lend itself to this more graphical representation.

Why Use Tables?

Use tables to shorten textual explanations. Determine the kinds of information contained in your report—e.g., definitions, commands, actions, benefits, and the like—and then arrange the information in a table. The table should eliminate unnecessarily repeated words and phrases and organize the material tightly.

The disadvantage of using tables is that tables contain only essential information without much amplification. This format may be too sketchy for some audiences.

Ordinarily, though, a table does the following:

• Shows relationships among information quickly
• Allows audiences to retrieve information more readily

- Permits more creative problem-solving, in that audiences can move through the levels of complexity and detail and still keep an eye on the big picture
- Permits faster scanning of information.

For writers, the tabular format allows

- Better analysis and updating of information by more readily revealing inconsistent, illogical, or outmoded information.
- More direct, crisper writing.

EXAMPLE—Standard Text

Let's look at one example of how standard text can be formatted in tabular form. First, look at this example of standard text:

When time is limited, travel by rocket, unless cost is also limited, in which case go by space ship. When only cost is limited, an astrobus should be used for journeys of less than 10 orbs, and a satellite for longer journeys. Cosmocars are recommended when there are no constraints on time or cost, unless the distance to be traveled exceeds 10 orbs. For journeys longer than 10 orbs, when time and cost are not important, journeys should be made by super star.

EXAMPLE—Tabular Text

Now let's see how the above text could be placed into tabular format to permit better understanding:

Limitations	If journey is less than 10 orbs, travel by . . .	If journey is more than 10 orbs, travel by . . .
Time	Rocket	Rocket
Cost	Astrobus	Satellite
None	Cosmocar	Super Star
Time and Cost	Space Ship	Space Ship

> Stop reading now and work through Exercises 8-2 and 8-3
> to practice converting information to a tabular format.

EXERCISE 8-2
(Individual)

Analyze the following information; then organize it into a tabular format.

3.0 ANTENNAS

The antenna arrangement (Figure 10-3) provides for a worst case configuration of 16 individual antenna structures, two of which serve multiple functions. Of these 16 individual antenna structures, six are attached to the payload skin or shroud, five are attached to the recovery bay skin, four are mounted directly to the internal payload structure and operate through windows or radomes, and one is mounted in the recovery system flotation gear. A brief summary of each of these antennas is provided in Table 10-5.

All antennas attached directly to vehicle skin use a compression type gasket to provide an electromagnetic interference (EMI)/water seal and to provide continuous conductivity between antenna back planes and vehicle skin. The six antenna structures attached to the payload shroud and their coaxial cable harnesses are removed with the shroud as an assembly. This design will require the disconnection of as many as eight coaxial cable connectors (worst case) at the shroud-to-vehicle attach point. When specific antenna systems are not required for a given mission, the vehicle will be configured with appropriate antenna "blanks" that are common.

3.1 Mounting Locations

The transmit antenna (Figure 10-15) is located 35 inches from the nose on the top centerline. It is a blade type antenna mounted from the inside of the shroud. The antenna

---

"ground plane" to the skin is accomplished by a metal impregnated tape which also functions as a sealing gasket between the antenna and the nose skin. Clearances to the nearest component is approximately 1.5 inches.

The scoring telemetry antenna (Figure 10-16) is located at station 135.0 on the bottom centerline. It is a blade antenna mounted from the inside of the shroud. Clearance to the nearest component is 2.0 inches, which is the scorer.

The altimeter antennas (Figure 10-17) are mounted on the bottom centerline of the vehicle. The forward antenna is located at station 152.5 in the payload section. The rear antenna is located at station 185.3 in the recovery bay. All are flush mounted to the skin from the outside. Clearance of the forward antenna to the nearest component is two inches. Clearance between the rear altimeter is approximately 0.40 inches and the recovery bay parachute compartment floor structure.

The Relay Reporter Responder drone control antennas (Figure 10-18) are located on the horizontal centerline at station 178.25, both right and left sides. They are flush-mounted in structural members of the recovery bay and are installed from the outside. The nearest interference point is the recovery bay structure. The signal ground plane is accomplished in the same manner as the other flush-mounted antenna.

The wrap antenna extends from station 159.0 to station 165.0 (Figure 10-19). It is flush with the skin and 15.6 inches in diameter. The antenna is opened sufficiently for the cable connections to clear the mounting surface at installation. The antenna is mounted on the aft end of the nose section on a machined ring which is permanently attached to the nose. This ring is also the O-ring sealing surface and the nose mounting interface for component maintenance.

The bistatic transmitter antenna (Figure 10-20) is located at station 164.0 on the vertical centerline far enough below the surface of the skin to clear the antenna window. The window is five inches wide and six inches long and is a 0.059 inches thick, permanently attached to the skin. The antenna has a three-bolt mounting pattern on the base for mounting to a support bracket which is attached to the component structure in the nose. The antenna is canted 45 degrees forward and remains with the payload structure intact when the nose cone is removed. Clearance to the nearest component is one inch.

The receive antennas are located on the left and right sides of the horizontal centerline (Figure 10-20). These antennas are canted forward 36 degrees and are mounted as close to the windows as possible. There is a three-hole tapped base plate for attaching to the mounting bracket, which is part of the payload structure. Clearance to the nearest component is approximately 0.30 inches. The windows are 3.25 inches long and 3.75 inches wide, and are sealed with a membrane 0.059 inches thick permanently attached to the skin.

The common destruct receiver antennas are located in the left and right wiring tunnels at station 185.3 on the horizontal centerline (Figure 10-21). These blade type antennas are 6 inches long, 0.5 wide and 0.93 high (Figure 10-22). Clearance to the nearest component (the drone antenna mounting frame) is 0.50 inches. The multifunction nose antenna is mounted to and supported by three structural members which extend forward from the payload structural bulkhead at station 130.0. This antenna is located in the forward part of the nose in the radome at station 122.0 (Figure 10-23). Clearance to the nearest component (the receive antenna) is 4.0 inches.

Take the information in Section B of the following text and convert it into a table.

DATA REDUCTION

A. Equipment

Figure 4 shows the equipment/setup used in reducing the recorded measurements into the psd, linear spectrum, and time history plots. Refer to "Tape Recorder/Spectrum Analyzer Description" section for description of these instruments. The plotter used was an HP-7550A 8-pen plotter.

B. Plot Description

All plots are gain on the y-axis and frequency on the x-axis. No phase information was processed in this report. The power spectral density (psd) plots have gain units in (engineering units)^2/Hz. The spectrum plots on the lower half of the page have gain units of RMS engineering units. The sample plot (figure 5) shows how to read the magnitude on the y-axis. The sample plot also shows what various characters represent with regard to the reduction of the data.

The spectrum plots (or linear spectrum) plots were obtained from the psd plots by multiplying the psd by the delta frequency used to reduce the data off the tape into the frequency domain. That result then was square rooted to produce the linear spectrum of the psd data. Thus the 'M' is recorded in the upper left of the linear spectrum plot.

The angualr positon plots were obtained from the angular acceleration data. The angular acceleration psd was artificially integrated by dividing each point on the plot by (2*PI*(the frequency corresponding to that point))4. This is the same principle as integrating sine and cosine functions.

The labels describing the plots include the orientation of the linear or angular measurement. For the linear measurements the orientation refers to vehicle coordinates: Lateral, Longitudinal, and Vertical. For the angular measurements the orientation refers to the LOS coordinate system: LOS Roll, LOS Pitch, LOS Yaw. Refer to the "Measurement Setup Descritption," section 13.

The Right Place, the Right Heading

Formatting Information

You may categorize information in a variety of formats, including the traditional textual format (paragraphs) and tables. Regardless of format, you must first classify information and then choose appropriate headings for the information.

9

Sort the Information

CONTENTS

Picking a Pattern

Work with Your Raw Information

Once you finish categorizing the information for your document, sort the information within each category into a pattern. That pattern may take the form of a hierarchy or some other arrangement. For instance, in the categorizing stage, I talked about the random notes that you collected:

- Buy carrots
- Buy shoelaces
- Buy potatoes
- Buy wine
- Buy lettuce
- Buy beer
- Buy Lean Cuisine frozen meals
- Have shoes fixed
- Take Andrew to his basketball game
- Fill prescription for dog's skin condition
- Take Sara to her ballet lesson
- Ice cream.

Select Your Categories

At the end of the week, you arranged those random notes into the following categories:

Supermarket   Kids' Activities   Drugstore   Liquor Store

Sort Within Your Categories

Now, it's time to sort the purchases in a pattern under each category. For example, under the category "Supermarket," you have

- Carrots
- Potatoes
- Lettuce
- Ice cream
- Lean Cuisine frozen meals
- Shoelaces.

If you are as slow as I am, it will take you one hour or longer to accomplish all the shopping. Then I may have some errands to run after that. Hence, I would purchase the least perishable products first and the most perishable last—so that foods would tend not to defrost in the car. I would impose the following order on my shopping list:

SUPERMARKETS

Shoelaces
Carrots
Potatoes
Lettuce
Lean Cuisine frozen meals
Ice cream

Think about sorting through all of the categories of your document in a similar way. Determine which pattern is best for the particular batch of information, and arrange the information accordingly.

What You Will Learn

This chapter presents Stage 5 of the TWP, sorting the information.

When you finish this chapter, you will

- Know the various patterns that you can use to arrange information
- Consciously arrange information in your documents according to the most appealing patterns.

Attitude Check

Before you begin reading this chapter, review the following attitudes discussed in Chapter 1 of this manual:

- Organize information as tightly as possible (p. 20).
- Use action titles (p. 20).
- Place important information at the front of the document (p. 21).

Organizational Patterns

Select a Pattern to Organize

Organizational patterns are schemes used to arrange information. There are no right or wrong patterns; however, certain patterns are more or less effective depending on your audience and the information you want to convey. Know your audience and your information—then choose the pattern that fits best.

Ten Typical Organizational Patterns

The following list of patterns is not complete, but it does show some of the more commonly used organizational patterns:

1. **Chronological**—Begins with the event that occurs first in time and continues to succeeding events.

   > On July 19, 1988, I discovered that the widgets we manufactured were undersized. We stopped producing the widgets immediately. On July 20, 1988, our quality control group met to discuss the deviation. In our meeting, we discovered . . . On July 21, we reported our findings to . . .

2. **Psychological**—The most important information is arranged in the most strategic place—sometimes at the beginning, sometimes at the end, or in any other strategic place. For example, executives are interested in profit and loss and want to see budgets up front. Engineers want to see technical information first.

3. **Spatial**—Describes a subject (for instance, the contents of a room) from the left to the right, top to bottom, near to far, etc., depending on the desired perspective.

   > A hypodermic needle is a slender, hollow, steel instrument used to introduce medication into the body. It is a single piece composed of three parts, all considered sterile: the hub, the cannula, and the point. The hub is the upper, larger part of the needle that attaches to the necklike opening on the syringe barrel. Next is the cannula (stem), the smooth and slender central portion. Last is the point, which consists of a beveled (slanted) opening, ending in a sharp tip.

4. **General to Specific**—Begins with a definition and leads to examples of the definition or begins with a conclusion or hypothesis and leads to supporting information.

> The Wankel engine has obvious advantages over the conventional V-8 engine. Its simplicity of design and operation adds to its efficiency and adaptability. The Wankel's lack of valves and camshaft—parts found in all conventional engines—increases its breathing abilities, making for a smooth running engine on low-octane gas. Because of its high power-to-weight ratio, the Wankel allows more passenger room in large automobiles, while providing better power and performance in smaller ones. Even the cost of manufacturing and maintaining the Wankel should be lower because of its few moving parts.

5. **Problem to Solution**—Begins with a problem and leads to the solution(s).

6. **Whole to Parts**—Begins with the hardware completely assembled and leads to the subassemblies.

> Television involves the transmission of scenes, either still or motion, by electrical means, most frequently for instantaneous viewing. Principal elements required for a television system include 1) a camera-type device to pick up the scene; 2) a transducer to convert the light impulses of the scene to a corresponding electrical signal; 3) a transmitter to convert the electrical signals into proper form for transmission to a distant receiver; 4) a receiver to pick up the transmitted signals and convert them to the proper form to apply to a further transducer; and 5) a transducer to convert the electrical signals back into light and, thus, reproduce the original scene.

7. **Most Important to Least Important**—Begins with the most important information and leads to the least important. You can delete extraneous material from the end if space does not allow you to include all information.

8. **Comparison/Contrast**—Discusses all facets of one alternative and then all facets of another alternative. Or discusses a facet of one alternative and then goes on to a facet of another alternative, maintaining this pattern throughout.

9. **Cause/Effect**—Begins with the cause of the situation and continues with the effect(s).

10. **New/Old Sentence Structure**—By new/old, I mean that authors should link information within sentences and also from one sentence to another. For example, in the sentence, "You may execute the command to delete by pressing the backspace key," both "command" and "backspace key" are new information which the audience has not previously seen. In a sentence following the first, "The backspace key is located in the upper right-hand corner of the keyboard," "backspace key" becomes old information and "keyboard" is new information. In a third sentence, "The keyboard in this computer configuration also contains a delete key which performs the same funtion as the backspace key," "keyboard" now becomes old information. This new/old pattern of linking information ensures a high degree of clarity.

A Note About These Patterns

Be especially mindful of the fact that, as a technical/scientific person, you are probably used to thinking and expressing yourself inductively—that is, moving from the specific to the general. This pattern is not necessarily best for audiences, since it saves conclusions, hypotheses, or recommendations for the end. Audiences usually want to know your hypothesis, conclusion, or recommendation *before* they read the document.

> Stop reading now and work through Exercise 9-1 to look more closely at how organizational patterns apply to your documents.

**EXERCISE 9-1
(Individual)**

Choose an organizational pattern for one category of information in your Writing Sample. Then sort the information within the category accordingly.

Be prepared to discuss your reasons for choosing the organizational pattern.

Sorting It Out

Remember Your Reader

Sorting is an important step toward proper organization of the information in your documents. When you sort, think about your audience. Who is the audience, and what rhetorical patterns of organization will most successfully appeal to the audience? Use of the proper organizational pattern can simplify your writing task and lead to a more readable document.

10 ·

Outline the Information

CONTENTS

Building the Structure

Outlining Your Information

Outlining is the fourth step in organizing information in a document. After you finish sorting the information in all of your categories, you should arrange the clusters of organized information into one overall appealing pattern, or scheme. When you do this, you have your outline.

Do not concern yourself with rules for outlining or outlining format. Use whatever format you like for your outline as long as it works.

What You Will Learn

This chapter presents Stage 6 of the TWP, outlining the information.

When you finish this chapter, you will

- Apply your knowledge of rhetorical patterns to the overall organization of information in your document
- Create an outline that will serve as a guide to creating an effective document
- Write a topic sentence/lead sentence for each major section of your outline.

Attitude Check

Before you begin reading this chapter, review the following attitudes discussed in Chapter 1 of this manual:

- Organize information as tightly as possible (p. 20).
- Use action titles (p. 20).
- Place important information at the front of the document (p. 21).
- Outline your documents (p. 23).

Introduction to Outlining

Overcome the Rules

In school, I disliked outlining for three reasons:

- I had to use Roman numerals, which I hadn't learned as well as I should have.

- I had to use a combination of Roman and Arabic numerals, plus upper- and lower-case letters, and it wasn't always easy to keep track of them.
- The teacher would not allow me or my classmates to have one subcategory under a major category. He/she said that I would have to integrate the subcategory into the major category.

When I freed myself from my teachers' scrutiny, I broke the "rules" of outlining and began to appreciate its advantages.

Use Your Own Outlining Style

Don't bog down in the rules of outlining. Do whatever works for you. Use Roman numerals or Arabic numerals or a decimal system, or don't use any numbers at all. But do arrange categories and the information within them according to patterns.

Keys to Successful Outlining

Outlining Solves Problems

Most writers do not outline. Perhaps they feel uncomfortable with it; perhaps they don't want to take the time necessary to plan their document. Nevertheless, outlining can solve many typical writing problems—often before the problems occur.

Proportion Problems

If you don't outline, you can't see the proportion among the various modules of your document. You may be too skinny here or too heavy there. When you outline, you can quickly see these problems.

Placement Problems

Outlining also solves the problem of writers placing the most important information last instead of first. Why do writers do this? Generally, it's because they don't really know what they will discuss until they finish discussing it. Reflexively, writers spill their guts first, paying little attention to the "spilling." Then they go back and "fix" the document.

Procrastination Problems

An outline allows you to begin writing a module or submodule and then finish it. When you return to your writing, you need not constantly search for a starting point. You can write section by section.

An outline also allows you to begin at any point—beginning, middle, or end—within a document. You can pick up wherever you feel most comfortable or most knowledgeable. Your knowledge becomes cumulative as you write. You'll find that those sections you felt you would write with difficulty now can be written with greater ease because your knowledge base has "snowballed."

Approval Problems

Be sure that a supervisor or colleague approves your outline before you start writing. Otherwise, you may miss the mark and not fulfill the expectations for the document. Nothing in writing is more disheartening than seeing your document severely criticized—or even discarded—because it takes the wrong approach or fails to meet necessary expectations. Always make sure your outline and general approach are approved by the appropriate decision-makers before you begin writing. When appropriate, show your outline to your supervisor and solicit comments on the content and arrangement. Then you can write, confident that the supervisor will approve of your attempts to communicate with your audience.

An Outline Guides You

When you finish your outline, tack it above your desk. Then let it guide you in creating order within your document. Your audience will benefit greatly from your attention to organization.

Just Communicate

Don't be too concerned about the style and format of your outline. Numbering and lettering, outline format, parallel construction— none of these are particularly important as long as your outline guides you and reflects the logic that will most effectively appeal to your audience.

Juice Up Your Outline

Audiences don't want dry, dusty, impersonal messages. Even in technical documents there is room for personal communication.

Lead Sentences

Consider expanding your outline to include lead or topic sentences. Lead sentences hook the reader into reading the sections of your document. Topic sentences alert readers to the subject of your discussion.

Whenever possible, use anecdotes (stories), dialogue, quotations, questions, analogies, and even statistics to add a personal flavor to your messages. Use any of these techniques in lead sentences, and add the sentences to your outline, as appropriate.

Look at the following examples to see how to add flavor to your text.

- Anecdotes

   I conducted a Preliminary Design Review for my committee on June 2. Before we began the session, the chief engineer said that he was lucky enough to have some very fine English teachers when he was in school. He remembered that Mrs. Brody taught very well. In fact, she encouraged students to write as concisely as possible. This statement undermined my argument that English teachers, generally, encouraged students to use long words and sentences whenever possible.

- Dialogue

   "I state in the Introduction that part of the reason students fail to write concisely relates to the impression created by English teachers. English teachers encouraged students to write long words and long sentences."

   "John, I'll take issue with that. Mrs. Brody, one of my favorite English teachers, encouraged us to write as concisely as possible."

- Quotations

   Alexander Pope, one of the great poets of the 18th Century, said, in his *Essay on Criticism,*

"Words are like leaves. Where they most abound,
Much fruit of sense beneath is rarely found."

- Questions

  What is one of the major roadblocks to your writing clear
  technical documents? If you answered verbosity, you spoke the
  truth.

- Analogies

  Using too many words to communicate your messages is like
  using too much salt in the stew. Pretty soon both the messages
  and the stew are unpalatable.

- Statistics

  Eighty percent of the engineers polled indicated that their primary
  problem in communicating was using too many words.

Topic Sentences

Topic sentences tip readers off to the subject of your paragraph,
summarize your subject, or introduce your subject. Topic
sentences present an overview of the information to come and
focus your audience's attention on the scope of your information.

Example of an Outline Format

Review the following example to see what an outline might look
like:

    1.0 The Four Subsystems of the Widget Produce the Desired Result
        1.1 Subsection 1 Senses the Target
                1.1.1 The Number of Sensors
                1.1.2 Location of the Sensors
        1.2 Subsection 2 Activates the Mechanism
        1.3 Subsection 3 . . .
    2.0 The Location of the . . .

Outliner Software

If you use a computer to write documents, try outliner
software—for instance, WordStar, PC Write, ThinkTank, etc.
Outliner software allows you to build your document from
scratch, to expand and collapse sections, and to write entire parts

of sections. The software isn't perfect, and it is not as user-friendly as I would like, but it is serviceable. We won't look at this software here, but I suggest that you try it.

> Stop reading now and work through Exercise 10-1 to learn more about outlining.

EXERCISE 10-1 (Individual)

1. Choose an overall pattern for all categories in your Writing Sample. Then create an outline. Be prepared to discuss your reasons for choosing a particular overall pattern.

2. Write a lead or topic sentence for each major section of your outline. Place the lead or topic sentence on the line below the action title of the major section.

Keeping On Track

Your Outline Brings It Together

When you complete your outline, you will have finished organizing your document. A solid outline serves as an invaluable guide to writing your document.

11

Design the Document

CONTENTS

First Impressions

What Makes a Document Difficult to Read?

Often, you can identify an effective document with only a glance. An ineffective document contains "wall-to-wall" text—text stretching from one narrow margin to another, bulky paragraphs that demand too much sustained attention from the audience, long sentences that leave the audience breathless, monotonous use of type styles and sizes, and poorly copied (faded) pages of text.

Also, the information in the report is difficult for the audience to find. In longer reports, the audience has difficulty finding sections, chapters, topics.

The Importance of Appearance

The foundations of a document are its technical accuracy and writing style. But an effective format invites the audience to examine the document's technical details and facilitates the speed with which audiences read documents.

Aesthetics Are Important

Well-designed hardware and software invite customers to explore them and become proficient in their use. The same can be said for well-designed, easy-to-read reports. Reports must reflect planning and an organized approach. They must be easy to use.

Like it or not, the aesthetics (bells and whistles) of a page determine to a great degree the interest readers develop in documents.

What You Will Learn

This chapter presents Stage 7 of the TWP, designing the document.

After you complete this chapter, you will

1. Use an abstract, glossary, and other front matter elements.
2. Use more vertical lists to display information. Learn conventions for vertical lists: punctuation, capitalization, highlights.
3. Use enumerated lists in paragraphs.
4. Write shorter sentences.
5. Use headers and footers in addition to page numbers.
6. Paragraph more frequently.
7. Break out information into more discrete sections and chapters.
8. Use more white space.
9. Use a two-column format.
10. Use "ragged right" text, instead of right-justified text.

Attitude Check

Before you begin reading this chapter, review the following attitude discussed in Chapter 1 of this manual:

- Keep most of your sentences short (p. 18).
- Use action titles (p. 20).
- Clear documentation takes time (p. 25).

Front Matter in Your Documents

Types of Front Matter

Use an abstract, table of contents, glossary, and other front matter elements to introduce audiences to the information in your documents. Supply audiences, up front, with information critical to their understanding of your document.

Abstracts

I cannot think of a document that would not benefit from an abstract. An abstract placed at the beginning of any document tells audiences

- The gist of the document
- Whether or not they need to read the document
- How much time they need to expend on this document.

An example of an abstract is provided on the following page.

Glossary

Writers usually place glossaries at the back of documents. I advocate placing glossaries at the front so that audiences will

- Know what they do not know
- Fill in those holes by reading the definitions *before* they read the text.

Table of Contents

Creating more sections or modules in your document will lead to a more detailed table of contents. Include all levels of headings in the table of contents so that audiences can have more specific access to your information.

SAMPLE ABSTRACT

AN ADVANCED, MODULAR,
INFRARED DATA
ACQUISITION
AND PROCESSING SYSTEM

APRIL 1985

TECHNICAL PUBLICATION

engineer:
document no.:
Keywords:

This paper describes a high-performance digital data acquisition and processing system for infrared sensors, using common-module detectors and their derivatives. The system is highly modular and has a wide range of potential applications to forward-looking infrared (FLIR) and infrared search/track (IRST) sensors. This hardware optimizes linear and nonlinear display image simultaneously, with an independent 10-bit dynamic range output for target trackers and screeners. Special integrated circuit (IC) and advanced packaging technology developments for high performance in a relatively small volume are also described. Hands-off image-optimization algorithms, test results, and efforts to improve sensor resolution are presented.

Vertical Lists

Advantages of Lists

Use vertical lists to display information. Take material buried in paragraphs and display it in a vertical list. Avoid excessive use of vertical lists, though, or your document will look like a grocery list.

Punctuating Lists

How do you punctuate, capitalize, and highlight information in a vertical list? Take your choice. If you follow traditional thinking, you will treat the list as part of a sentence and punctuate accordingly:

Testing the LOAL simulator on distorted imagery resulted in the following observations:

- the LOAL simulator is robust to horizontal shift, but performance degrades with vertical shift;
- rotation typically affects only those targets away from the image center;
- the LOAL simulator can tolerate large amounts of channel normalization gain error;
- poorer performance is obtained on images with small targets and on images with low contrast; and
- performance with the MDTRL is much better than performance with the MFS alone.

If you follow the tradition of marketeers and want to focus even more intensely on the items in the list, you might handle the capitalization and punctuation in the following way:

Testing the LOAL simulator on distorted imagery resulted in the following observations:

- The LOAL simulator is robust to horizontal shift, but performance degrades with vertical shift.
- Rotation typically affects only those targets away from the image center.
- Etc. . . .

Numbered Lists

Using Numbered Lists

You can use enumerated lists in paragraphs as alternatives to burying information in a paragraph or having too many vertical lists.

How Numbered Lists Can Help

Look at the following sentence:

Generally, processor capacity estimates are more difficult to make with real-time software systems because inputs may not be predictable, the load on the system may vary with time, or different events will require different operations, producing permutations of many simultaneous activities.

The author wrote the sentence well but could have highlighted the important items in the list by enumerating them. The author also could have avoided the ambiguity caused by the comma in the last item. In the rewritten sentence below, the author alerts the audience that a list is on the way.

Generally, processor capacity estimates are more difficult to make with real-time software systems because 1) inputs may not be predictable; 2) the load on the system may vary with time; or 3) different events will require different operations, producing many permutations of simultaneous activities.

Shorter Sentences

Keep It Short

Write shorter sentences. Longer sentences leave you breathless, literally, because we tend to pronounce all of our words when we read.

Look at an Example

Look at the following sentence:

> Since the gimbal was pointing down during maneuvers, indicating the gimbal was against its stop, it seems that a notable bias was introduced in the loop electronics, driving the gimbal against its stop and, therefore, not able to travel farther to null the gyro pickoff.

Say It a Better Way

The above sentence is understandable but not crisply expressed. Even if you know the subject and are a tolerant audience, such sentences take more time for your to read and comprehend. See if the following paragraph is easier to read:

> A notable bias, introduced in the loop electronics, drove the gimbal against its stop. In this position, the gimbal could not travel farther to null the gyro pickoff.

Choppy Isn't Bad

What's wrong with a choppy style? Look at the following paragraph:

> The system features four menus. Each menu contains six options. There are no submenus. You can move between options with a single keystroke. Also, you can exit the system from all menus and screens.

Does the choppiness offend you? Does it impede your understanding of the information?

> Stop reading now and work through Exercise 11-1 to practice working with short sentences.

EXERCISE 11-1 (Individual)

Convert the following long sentences to shorter ones.

1. After the installation of the DYMPAC to the inner gimbal in place of the FLIR assembly, the inner gimbals were balanced by the hand-eye technique (tossing lightly the gimbal to and fro, and studying the gimbal motion to determine what side of the rotating axis was the unbalance).

2. When the gimbal system was pointing forward and level the DYMPAC x-axis was pointing to the port and level or lined up in the vehicle lateral direction, the y-axis pointing forward and level or in the logitudinal direction, the z-axis is pointing up or in the vertical direction.

Headers and Footers

Why Use Headers and Footers?

Use headers and footers in addition to page numbers on as many documents as possible so that audiences can more readily identify the contents of a page.

Look at the two examples on the following pages to see how headers and footers can help the audience identify the contents of a page—thus, better orienting the reader within the document.

EXAMPLE—Document without Headers and Footers

Shell Variables

In addition to the login script file, DNIX provides other facilities for environment customization, known as shell variables. User-configurable shell variables include HOME, your home (login) directory, and PATH, your command search path (a concept identical to the MS-DOS path). Shell variables may be passed from a parent process to a child process but never in the other direction.

File System

The Daisy-DNIX file system is a hierarchical structure designed to handle many data management tasks. Within the file system, there are two main forms of data organization: directories and terminal files (also simply called files). Because the file structure is hierarchical, it may be visualized as a tree, with branches (directories) and leaves (files). A file is a collection of data, either binary or ASCII. A directory is a collection of files and/or directories grouped together for some arbitary reason. There is no limit (other than available disk space) to the number of hierarchical levels in the tree. The maximum number of entries in any directory is 288, but a practical and reasonable limit is 24 because of the way in which DNIX manages its files. Some of the more important directories and files are identified on the next page.

A very important features of the Daisy-DNIX file system is that unlike PC-based operating systems such as MS-DOS, the file structure is based entirely on logical relationships. Physical storage devices are linked into the file system through directories, rather than being identified as physically separate. Thus at the shell level there are no references to drives when specifying file locations. It is analogous to a single large disk drive in the MS-DOS world.

EXAMPLE—Document with Headers and Footers

Shell Variables

In addition to the login script file, DNIX provides other facilities for environment customization, known as shell variables. User-configurable shell variables include HOME, your home (login) directory, and PATH, your command search path (a concept identical to the MS-DOS path). Shell variables may be passed from a parent process to a child process but never in the other direction.

File System

The Daisy-DNIX file system is a hierarchical structure designed to handle many data management tasks. Within the file system, there are two main forms of data organization: directories and terminal files (also simply called files). Because the file structure is hierarchical, it may be visualized as a tree, with branches (directories) and leaves (files). A file is a collection of data, either binary or ASCII. A directory is a collection of files and/or directories grouped together for some arbitrary reason. There is no limit (other than available disk space) to the number of hierarchical levels in the tree. The maximum number of entries in any directory is 288, but a practical and reasonable limit is 24 because of the way in which DNIX manages its files. Some of the more important directories and files are identified on the next page.

A very important features of the Daisy-DNIX file system is that unlike PC-based operating systems such as MS-DOS, the file structure is based entirely on logical relationships. Physical storage devices are linked into the file system through directories, rather than being identified as physically separate. Thus at the shell level there are no references to drives when specifying file locations. It is analogous to a single large disk drive in the MS-DOS world.

Paragraphing

Give Your Audience a Break

Paragraph more to relieve the fatigue audiences experience comprehending heavyweight paragraphs. Let your eyes fall on these two paragraphs:

Most current symbolic systems implement garbage collection using incremental or generational algorithms or some combination of the two. The generational garbage collection techniques appear to be the most amenable to real-time systems. The two major bottlenecks in garbage collection are the identification of live objects and the copying of these objects. In generational garbage collection, the pointers to live objects are remembered when they are created so that the garbage collector has this information available when it executes. Since the theory behind generational GC is that newly created objects tend to become garbage quickly, the copying problem is somewhat alleviated by frequent collections of the youngest objects. The copying of objects can induce a critical region in the system that excludes the execution of any process that uses garbage collection and therefore adds a latency factor to any event being handled by a garbage-collected process. However, in a fighter aircraft with its high data rate, it may be necessary to divide the system into two domains, one that has implicit garbage collection, and the other that is not garbage-collected. In such a system, any event response constraints that cannot be met with the garbage collection latency must either generate no garbage or manage their own memory resources.

The basic system software is independent of the language and architecture. The chosen language will most likely require its own run-time additions to the system software to support language constructs. It has been speculated that not only could AI languages such as Lisp be supported with real-time system software, but that the inference languages could also be supported. For example, inference languages could be treated as instances of symbolic programming languages, and inference engines as specialized instances of run-time systems. The rule languages used to encode expert knowledge into a knowledge base has an explicit syntax, with semantic content that may be derived by compiling. In current expert systems, the inference engine interpretively executes the rules, providing specialized support for run-time dependent variables (the working memory elements). The rule and working memory elements definitions are unique for each expert system developed, but the inference engine (run-time environment) that allows rules to execute remains the same. This theory is of pivotal importance to the outcome of this study, because it would aid in achieving the desired goal of moving the application closer to the hardware and thereby improving system performance.

A Better Way

Now evaluate this rendering of the same information divided into six paragraphs:

Most current symbolic systems implement garbage collection using incremental or generational algorithms or some combination of the two. The generational garbage collection techniques appear to be the most amenable to real-time systems. The two major bottlenecks in garbage collection are the identification of live objects and the copying of these objects. In generational garbage collection, the pointers to live objects are remembered when they are created so that the garbage collector has this information available when it executes.

Since the theory behind generational GC is that newly created objects tend to become garbage quickly, the copying problem is somewhat alleviated by frequent collections of the youngest objects. The copying of objects can induce a critical region in the system that excludes the execution of any process that uses garbage collection and therefore adds a latency factor to any event being handled by a garbage-collected process.

However, in a fighter aircraft with its high data rate, it may be necessary to divide the system into two domains, one that has implicit garbage collection, and the other that is not garbage-collected. In such a system, any event response constraints that cannot be met with the garbage collection latency must either generate no garbage or manage their own memory resources.

The basic system software is independent of the language and architecture. The chosen language will most likely require its own run-time additions to the system software to support language constructs.

It has been speculated that not only could AI languages such as Lisp be supported with real-time system software, but that the inference languages could also be supported. For example, inference languages could be treated as instances of symbolic programming languages, and inference engines as specialized instances of run-time systems. The rule languages used to encode expert knowledge into a knowledge base has an explicit syntax, with semantic content that may be derived by compiling. In current expert systems, the inference engine interpretively executes the rules, providing specialized support for run-time dependent variables (the working memory elements).

The rule and working memory elements definitions are unique for each expert system developed, but the inference engine (run-time environment) that allows rules to execute remains the same. This theory is of pivotal importance to the outcome of this study, because it would aid in achieving the desired goal of moving the application closer to the hardware and thereby improving system performance.

Making It Even Clearer

Another wrinkle—use action titles, too:

Generational Garbage Collection Techniques
Are Superior to Incremental Techniques

Most current symbolic systems implement garbage collection using incremental or generational algorithms or some combination of the two. The generational garbage collection techniques appear to be the most amenable to real-time systems. The two major bottlenecks in garbage collection are the identification of live objects and the copying of these objects. In generational garbage collection, the pointers to live objects are remembered when they are created so that the garbage collector has this information available when it executes.

Alleviating Copying Problems

Since the theory behind generational GC is that newly created objects tend to become garbage quickly, the copying problem is somewhat alleviated by frequent collections of the youngest objects. The copying of objects can induce a critical region in the system that excludes the execution of any process that uses garbage collection and therefore adds a latency factor to any event being handled by a garbage-collected process.

High Data Rate May Necessitate Dividing the System

However, in a fighter aircraft with its high data rate, it may be necessary to divide the system into two domains, one that has implicit garbage collection, and the other that is not garbage-collected. In such a system, any event response constraints that cannot be met with the garbage collection latency must either generate no garbage or manage their own memory resources.

The Language of the System

The basic system software is independent of the language and architecture. The chosen language will most likely require its own run-time additions to the system software to support language constructs.

The System Can Support Inference Language

It has been speculated that not only could AI languages such as Lisp be supported with real-time system software, but that the inference languages could also be supported. For example, inference languages could be treated as instances of symbolic programming languages, and inference engines as specialized instances of run-time systems. The rule languages used to encode expert knowledge into a knowledge base has an explicit syntax, with semantic content that may be derived by compiling. In current expert systems, the inference engine interpretively executes the rules, providing specialized support for run-time dependent variables (the working memory elements).

The Theory of Rule and Working Memory Elements

The rule and working memory elements definitions are unique for each expert system developed, but the inference engine (run-time environment) that allows rules to execute remains the same. This theory is of pivotal importance to the outcome of this study, because it would aid in achieving the desired goal of moving the application closer to the hardware and thereby improving system performance.

Modules

Allowing Easier Access to Information

Break out information into more discrete subsections, sections, and chapters. This allows the audience speedier access to the specifics of your reports. Again, beware of making your reports look fragmented. But wherever a natural break in the subject occurs, consider creating a new module.

> Stop reading now and work through Exercise 11-2 to practice breaking text into modules.

EXERCISE 11-2 (Individual)

Read the passage on this page and the following two pages and break out the information into multiple subsections.

SECTION SEVEN: MILLIMETER WAVE SYSTEM SUMMARY

7.0 SUMMARY

Millimeter waves can be viewed as having less attenuation effects from weather than laser wavelengths and smaller beamwidths than microwaves. Perhaps it is a better view to say, millimeter waves have larger beamwidths and less accuracy than lasers and more signal attenuation than microwaves! Millimeter systems fall in the middle of the spectrum that has been investigated and this generally results in middle of the road performance as well.

Angular accuracy and resolution can be found using Equations 7.1 and 7.2. For a 95 GHz system, representative values for Ω and ρ are approximately 10 mrads or .6°, and 8 to 10 meters. As mentioned in the performance requirements section, this is adequate for the OW mission.

Equation 7.1

$$\Omega = 1.25 \, (\lambda/D)$$

Where Ω = Angular accuracy
λ = Wavelength
D = Aperture diameter

Equation 7.2

$$\rho = C\tau/2$$

Where ρ = Range resolution
C = speed of light
τ = pulse width

Due to the smaller beamwidths, millimeter systems are more covert and perform the OW mission better than microwave systems. Low level detection will be improved by a reduction in multipath, glint, and specular reflections. Also, reduced off-axis emissions and larger power density dissipation will reduce the chances of signal interception

---

and the resultant application of electronic counter-measures (ECM).

While millimeter waves are attenuated more in clear air and weather than microwaves, they penetrate smoke/obscurants equally well. Therefore, they overcome at least one atmospheric obstacle present with shorter wavelengths (i.e., lasers).

Millimeter wave technology, however, is less mature than microwaves or lasers. While the components are generally smaller than for microwaves, higher precision manufacturing is required. In addition, the receiver noise figures are higher, source efficiencies and stabilization are lower, and waveguide capabilities are inferior. And as with any new technology, manufacturing costs are higher.

System cost is higher, and system resolution and technological maturity are lower than for laser systems. However, longer detection ranges due to better transmission, higher peak power capabilities, and larger scan volume coverage makes millimeter waves a better candidate for the OW system. Table 7.1 summarizes the comparison of millimeter wave systems to microwaves and lasers.

Table 7.1
Comparison of Microwave, Millimeter Wave,
and Laser Systems

CHARACTERISTIC	MICROWAVE	MILLIMETER WAVE	LASER
Accuracy/Resolution	Poor	Fair/Good	Good
Covertness	Poor	Fair	Good
Transmission (Clear Air)	Good	Fair	Poor
Transmission (Weather)	Good	Fair	Poor
Transmission (Smoke)	Good	Good	Poor
Volume Coverage	Good	Good	Poor
Component Size	Poor	Fair	Good
Component Availability	Good	Poor	Fair
Maturity/Empirical Data	Good	Poor	Good

> Most of the "Goods" are in the microwave and laser columns. As was mentioned at the top of this section, the millimeter system strikes a compromise between the advantages and disadvantages of microwave and laser systems. While theoretically capable of fulfilling the OW role, the biggest problems for millimeter wave systems are the technological immaturity and a limited amount of empirical data supporting analysis.

White Space

White Space = Readability

White space is an important factor in enhancing the readability of a document. We can increase white space by

- Widening the margins of a document
- Skipping lines between paragraphs
- Using space-and-a-half or double spacing between all lines
- Using a two-column format and reserving the left-hand column for headings only
- Breaking out information into more, discrete sections and using action titles to introduce those sections.

See the Difference

Compare the two documents on the following pages. The first contains a crowded, wall-to-wall text format. The second shows the same information in a different format with more white space.

EXAMPLE—Wall-to-Wall Format

Believe it or not, it has been more than a year since we first talked about a manuscript. I hope that your work has gone well. Mine certainly has. The technical writing program continues to grow. This fall we will enroll more than 700 students in 30 sections of technical writing. There are many reasons for our growth. One important one is that Computer Sciences has allowed its majors two new options: 1) to elect the beginning Technical Writing course rather than the second half of Freshman English, and 2) to substitute three advanced technical writing courses for three foreign language courses. When we last talked, I suggested to you that two "holes" in the market existed. First, technical writing needs a textbook for beginners—students and instructors. (The vast majority of instructors are teaching the course without benefit of experience in the field. These staff know what Freshman Composition is but not Technical Writing. Consequently, they need guidance, too.) Most texts are over-written and encyclopedic—they address the intricacies of various technical writing forms but do not explain the basic technical writing process. Second, the field needs a text or a secondary source on the technical editing process. Please keep the second book in mind because I want to send you some material on that soon. For now, though, I will limit this correspondence to a beginning technical writing text. After directing the technical writing (TW) program for the last four years, I have gathered and written enough material to develop a text targeted at students in their first TW course. I have tentatively titled the book, Beginning Technical Writing. My book differs from other texts in its focus. First, *Beginning Technical Writing* focuses on the technical writing process as it occurs in the workplace with an emphasis on problem solving, research, organization, and review. Students apply the process to all their writing in the course.

EXAMPLE—New Format with White Space

Believe it or not, it has been more than a year since we first talked about a manuscript. I hope that your work has gone well. Mine certainly has. The technical writing program continues to grow. This fall we will enroll more than 700 students in 30 sections of technical writing. There are many reasons for our growth. One important one is that Computer Sciences has allowed its majors two new options: 1) to elect the beginning Technical Writing course rather than the second half of Freshman English, and 2) to substitute three advanced technical writing courses for three foreign language courses.

When we last talked, I suggested to you that two "holes" in the market existed. First, technical writing needs a textbook for beginners—students and instructors. (The vast majority of instructors are teaching the course without benefit of experience in the field. These staff know what Freshman Composition is but not Technical Writing. Consequently, they need guidance, too.) Most texts are over-written and encyclopedic—they address the intricacies of various technical writing forms but do not explain the basic technical writing process. Second, the field needs a text or a secondary source on the technical editing process. Please keep the second book in mind because I want to send you some material on that soon. For now, though, I will limit this correspondence to a beginning technical writing text.

After directing the technical writing (TW) program for the last four years, I have gathered and written enough material to develop a text targeted at students in their first TW course. I have tentatively titled the book, Beginning Technical Writing. My book differs from other texts in its focus.

First, *Beginning Technical Writing* focuses on the technical writing process as it occurs in the workplace with an emphasis on problem solving, research, organization, and review. Students apply the process to all their writing in the course.

Two-Column Format

Why a Two-Column Format?

Use a two-column format, placing your headings and subheadings in the narrower, left-hand column and placing text in the right-hand column. The headings and subheadings act as mini-abstracts for the associated text to their right. Each heading and its text is a "bite" of information.

This two-column format also allows audiences to glance vertically down the left-hand column and decide what to read and what to ignore.

Which Do You Prefer?

MTW has a two-column format. Compare it to the single-column sample that follows to see which is more appealing.

SAMPLE—Single-Column Format

Systems Department and this organization has been communicating with other Ada repositories nationwide. Therefore before designing or implementing any code, a library search to see if it already exists is appropriate.

The Ada reusability working group is defining methodological practices and standards which, when published, will further set guidelines for software coding to more fully capitalize on software reusability.

4.3 PRELIMINARY DESIGN

Preliminary design, or top-level design, is the development phase which translates the requirements into a definition of the relationships among software units and the hierarchy of control for the software. Thus, the data flow through the system becomes defined. This definition is documented in the Software Top Level Design Document (refer to paragraph 4.1.6, Documentation). System data flow definition may be in any form as long as the method chosen communicates clearly the intended structure of the software.

During this phase, each major software unit (module) and data and control interfaces between the modules are defined. Also, the Software Test Plan should be written to define the total scope of the software testing in support of software development.

The preliminary design phase may involve several design iterations before an acceptable design is presented at the Preliminary Design Review (PDR). On the other hand, design Iterations may result because of problems found during the PDR. This last scenario, however, should be avoided. It is naturally better if design iterations occur prior to the PDR since these iterations are essentially transparent to the customer.

4.3.1 TIMING CONSIDERATIONS

During preliminary design, timing constraints must be developed for software units. In real time systems, this frequently means allocating percentages of the available time to particular software units. It should also be determined whether or not adequate processing resources are available. If not, then either a faster processor must be used, more processors must be used, the requirements must be relaxed, or possibly a different language such as assembly language must be used.

Timing estimates should be as accurate as possible since more or faster processors typically add considerable cost to the final system. Time critical code is an excellent candidate for prototyping. In this way, timing that is difficult to estimate can be measured.

Ragged Right

Ragged Right Is More Readable

Studies of readability show that audiences read "ragged right"—irregular, unjustified lines of prose—more easily than right-justified lines.

See for Yourself

Here's an example of ragged right text:

An example of a traditional simple algorithm is the fixed priority scheme where processes execute within hierarchical priority domains. The more important processes execute in the higher priority domains and take precedence over processes in lower domains. A higher priority process will preempt a lower priority process when activated, even though the preempted process may currently be more time-critical.

Now see how the same text looks when it is right-justified:

An example of a   traditional simple algorithm is the   fixed priority scheme where processes execute within hierarchical priority domains. The more important processes execute in the   higher priority domains and   take precedence over processes in lower domains. A higher priority process will   preempt a lower priority process when   activated, even though the   preempted process may currently be more time-critical.

Notice the monotony of right-justified text and the spaces that some word processing programs insert in order to achieve the right justification.

Getting the Look

An Aid to Understanding

A pleasing format advances the understanding of text. Formatting should never be an afterthought or the last thing you consider when writing. Formatting is one of the keys to clear technical prose.

12 ·

Write the Document

CONTENTS

The Least Important Stage

An Automatic Process

Writing is the "least important" stage of the Technical Writing Process. It should occur automatically.

You have spent much of your time evaluating your audience, formulating tactics to appeal to the audience, gathering information, and organizing the information. Now, simply place your pen on the paper, or put your fingers on the keyboard, and let fly.

When you finish writing, all that remains is revising. We will discuss revising in Stage 9 of the TWP, covered in Part 4, Chapters 13–17.

Writing should be automatic. Is it? It can be, if you see writing in the proper perspective and adopt a relaxed approach. For instance, has any instructor of writing asked you to write as you speak? I advise you to do so.

What You Will Learn

This chapter presents Stage 8 of the TWP, writing.

When you finish this chapter, you will

- Write more quickly, more conversationally, and more personally
- Write section by section
- Write only, and not revise as you write.

Attitude Check

Before you begin reading this chapter, review the following attitudes discussed in Chapter 1 of this manual:

- Writing is problem solving (p. 15).
- Don't mimic the style of "experts" in the field (p. 16).
- Inject your own personality into your writing (p. 16).
- Keep most of your sentences short (p. 18).
- Write most of your sentences in natural word order (p. 18).
- Use the more readily understood word whenever possible (p. 19).
- Less is more (p. 19).

- Repeat nouns to avoid ambiguity (p. 20).
- Show your ignorance—ignorance is required (p. 21).
- Paper is only a vehicle for communicating our messages (p. 22).
- Writing clear documents takes great skill (p. 25).

Steps to Easier Writing

Writing Solves Problems

Writing is problem solving. Particular documents solve particular problems: training manuals solve the problems of teaching skills to participants. Proposals solve the software, hardware, or services problems that customers encounter.

Particular writing strategies and techniques solve other problems. For example, procedures aid others in repeating processes. Descriptions show others what widgets look like. Analogies make the unfamiliar familiar for uninformed audiences.

Improve Your Writing Speed

Improve the speed with which you problem-solve/write and the clarity of your expression by

1. Filing notes in a three-ring binder
2. Using boilerplate
3. Using models of previous documents
4. Writing as you speak
5. Writing section by section
6. Writing, not revising.

File Notes in a Three-Ring Binder

A Handy Organizational Tool

This is such a helpful tactic that I can't emphasize it enough. Simply keep a three-ring binder for your document and use it to store and organize your information. When I begin a three-ring binder for a project, I have a sense of being on the road, of having started the project—even though I may have only dividers and a few pages in the binder.

Use Boilerplate

Don't Reinvent the Wheel

Boilerplate is text that can be inserted in a number of different types of documents—sometimes with few, if any, changes.

Boilerplate text can include descriptions of facilities and equipment, company history and philosophy, resumes—any information that remains constant and is repeated in a number of documents.

Some companies capture all of their boilerplate and make it available to communicators so that communicators are not constantly reinventing the wheel.

Remember, adapt boilerplate to the audience and purpose of your document.

Use Models of Previous Documents

Examples to Go By

Model the format and substance of documents that others have used in appropriate circumstances. Create your own file of model documents that you regularly use.

Write as You Speak

A Conversational Approach

We're not used to putting thoughts down on paper in the same manner that we explain our ideas orally. We write stilted prose, using passive voice verbs and other awkward constructions. We can learn to revise our work and rephrase the most awkward passages, but another strategy is just to relax and "explain orally," as you write.

Imagine that a friend has dropped by and you are explaining the message in the document you must write. Simply write the document as you would if you were explaining it to your friend.

When you write as you speak, do not concern yourself with the "ooh's" and "aah's" that appear in the transcription of the draft. Don't bog down in the passive voices or awkward constructions that may inadvertently occur. You can revise later and achieve the consistency and formality you need.

Write Section by Section

One Step at a Time

Write section by section. Begin anywhere in your outline. Choose a section or subsection, one that will take 30–45 minutes to write. Then sit down and write it beginning to end. Open and closed. You've finished one segment of your document. No need to go back and remind yourself what you wrote and what is to come.

You've closed the book on one aspect of the document and can advance to another segment.

Tips for Relaxation

Take short breaks from your writing. Walk around your building—indoors if the weather is inclement, outdoors whenever possible. Fill your lungs with fresh air. Walking clears your mind and may stimulate good ideas for you to use in your writing. Someone once said, "Don't trust an idea you got by the seat of your pants."

Talk with a colleague to distract yourself for a few minutes. The distraction rests your mind.

Jog or walk at lunch or after work to clear and rest your mind. Writing documents is taxing, "heavyweight" work and demands periodic refreshment.

Write—Don't Revise

Don't Block Your Creativity

Remember, as you write your "write as you speak" draft, you are engaging in two separate activities—writing and revising. Always keep these activities separate. Writing involves capturing information—in that sense, it is similar to brainstorming. On the other hand, revising involves polishing the written information so that it reads clearly.

When you write, you capture information. Don't worry about polishing your words. Don't waste time reworking usage, punctuation, spelling, and capitalization. If you stop to rework, you may lose thoughts related to your topic.

I know it's hard not to revise as you write. You want to set things right as quickly as possible. But you'll find that if you resist the temptation to "edit on the fly," you'll be able to present more of your information clearly without encountering the dreaded "writer's block."

> Stop reading now and work through Exercise 12-1 to practice "writing as you speak."

**EXERCISE 12-1
(Individual)**

Following your Writing Sample outline, "write as you speak" two longer sections of the outline using a tape recorder or a dictating machine.

When you finish dictating the two sections, transcribe them, triple-spacing your draft.

Just Do It

Write Automatically

Writing should be the easiest stage in the TWP. It should be automatic. The more conversationally you write, the more easily you will write. Be a "lazy" writer. Do not reinvent the wheel. Use boilerplate and models. Write smart.

PART

4

Revise the Document

CONTENTS

Revising—The Road To Clarity

Polishing Your Text

Once you have completed the first draft of your document, you are ready to revise the document—to polish your text so that it is as clear and crisp as possible. Revising your document entails a variety of skills, which are discussed in five segments of Part 4.

What You Will Learn

This part presents Stage 9 of the TWP, revising your document.

In this part, you will become familiar with five crucial aspects of revising documents:

- Preferring active voice to passive voice (Chapter 13)
- Strengthening verbs (Chapter 14)
- Eliminating jargon (Chapter 15)
- Keeping text concise (Chapter 16)
- Writing professional documents (Chapter 17).

Attitude Check

Before you begin reading this part, review the following attitudes discussed in Chapter 1 of this manual:

- Don't mimic the style of "experts" in the field (p. 16).
- Inject your own personality into your writing (p. 16).
- Keep most of your sentences short (p. 18).
- Write most of your sentences in natural word order (p. 18).
- Use the more readily understood word whenever possible (p. 19).
- Less is more (p. 19).
- Repeat nouns to avoid ambiguity (p. 20).
- Organize information as tightly as possible (p. 20).

13 ·

Active Vs. Passive

CONTENTS

Using Verbs That Speak

Definition—Passive and Active

Passive voice grammatical constructions contain subjects that *do not* act. Active voice grammatical constructions contain subjects that *do* act.

Writers who use the passive voice maintain that in technical/ scientific writing the object of the action is usually more important than the actor. In order to emphasize the importance of the object, these writers place the object first—in the place of the subject—in the sentence.

The Advantage of Active Voice

Using passive voice is not grammatically incorrect. However, if you use more active voice verbs in your writing, your audiences can understand your documents more readily.

An Example

Let's try a simple experiment. Say to yourself, "The ball was kicked by me." You saw the ball, but it was not until later in your thought process that you realized that the ball was being kicked and who was doing the kicking.

Now repeat this sentence to yourself: "I kicked the ball." You quickly saw yourself approach the ball and boot it through the uprights. Simplistically, this example illustrates the difference between passive and active voice. Active voice tends to bring meaning closer to the front of the sentence so that audiences can comprehend meaning more quickly and easily.

Small Investment, Big Dividends

Use of active voice is crucial to development of a technical writing style that communicates. If we can convert passive voice verbs to active voice verbs, we will be expending only a little effort—but we'll find that this little effort will yield big results in terms of increasing clarity in writing.

Vilfredo Pareto, Italian sociologist and economist, formulated the principle that we can accomplish 80 percent of any task with 20 percent of the effort.

You can apply this to developing a clear technical writing style in the following way. If you learn to identify the passive voice and then convert the passive voice constructions in your documents to active voice, you will clear most of the obscurities from your documents.

Major Issue Involving Passive Voice

I hear many writers say, "When I write documents for the government, I must use passive voice." Not true. Nowhere in any government specification—or military standard—is there a requirement to use passive voice. In fact, the opposite is true. Government specifications and military standards recommend and require active voice and other language-saving techniques. Unfortunately, government evaluators are accustomed to writers using passive voice. Writers, in turn, now assume that evaluators want to continue the custom of using passive voice.

Most of the time, active voice will more clearly express your ideas. For example, both of the following sentences are grammatically correct:

- The operations manual was written by Tom Jones.
- Tom Jones wrote the operations manual.

The second sentence more effectively conveys the message because the key content words are closer to the front of the sentence, because the subject acts, and because the sentence is shorter and more quickly read. Note in the first sentence that the verb is concise, direct, and vigorous and that the action of the sentence is not drawn out and stilted.

Don't Force the Action

Parenthetically, we should never force the use of active voice. For instance, if we do not know who the actor is and cannot reasonably infer the actor, we should use the passive voice.

What You Will Learn

In this chapter, you will learn to

1. Discriminate between active and passive voice.
2. Demonstrate the appropriate use of active and passive voice.
3. Convert passive voice verbs to active voice verbs.

4. Delete extraneous prepositional phrases and other words—through increased use of active voice.
5. Identify the false and true subjects of sentences.
6. Place the true subject—the actor—first in the natural word order of a sentence and then follow the subject with the predicate, and, finally, the object.
7. Use natural word order in as many sentences as possible.

Why Worry About Active and Passive Voice?

Verbs Communicate Meaning

Verbs are words or phrases that activate the meaning of sentences.

Correct use of verbs plays a major role in developing a concise technical writing style. Verbs dominate meaning. They determine how well sentences, sections, and chapters communicate. Verbs control the amount of meaning audiences derive from sentences and the speed with which audiences derive that meaning.

Research into Passive Voice

In 1986, I conducted research into the use of passive and active voices. The study involved 100 undergraduate students who had no experience with word processing. Most of them had no experience with computers.

I extracted information from a WordStar manual and rewrote the information in three different ways:

- Using passive voice constructions exclusively
- Using active voice constructions exclusively
- Using mixed voice.

I gave one-third of the student sample the passive voice selection to read, one-third the active voice selection, and the final third the mixed voice selection to read. After each student read the extract, I administered the same 10-question test to each of the students. Then I asked them each to perform the same three rudimentary word processing tasks.

Those students who read the active voice selection correctly answered one question more than the others. Additionally, those who read the active voice selection performed the three word processing tasks in one minute less time than the others.

Example: Passive Voice

Read the following passage taken from a software manual. Note the many passive voice constructions. Don't evaluate the content of the passage. Merely record your reactions as you read along. Consider the following questions as you read.

- Are you bored?
- Are you confused?
- Did the passage enlighten you?
- Are you energized? Fatigued?
- Are you picking up the information quickly?
- Is the author getting to the point?
- What is the reason for all of this prose?
- Am I deciphering rather than reading?

The entry screens *are formatted* for each transaction with descriptive field names to assist the entry operator through each function *to be performed*. Information *may be entered* in any sequence and by several operators at different terminals. Prior to the nightly batch processing cycle, all transactions *are sorted* into the logical sequence *required* by the system.

In addition to the standard on-line entry features, transactions which *have been entered* during the day *can be viewed* on-line for verification. If a change *is required* for an unprocessed transaction, the change *can be made* at once or the transaction *can be deleted,* if desired.

At the completion of the nightly batch process, a list of all processed transactions is available for a hard copy report or *may be placed* on tape, micro-film, or fiche. Errors detected during the batch process *are reported* on an error listing report, *sequenced* in logical order and identifying the terminal operator and location. Transactions containing errors *are retained* by the system and *may be corrected* by simply re-keying the fields in error. Corrected transactions *are* automatically *included* in the next batch cycle.

What Did You Read?

Who or what are the actors in the above passage?

Does the fact that actors do not appear in the passage increase the efficiency with which the writer communicates the message?

How many words in the passage are extraneous to its message?

Example: Active Voice

The following passage is a rewritten version of the previous passage, with active voice verbs (italicized) substituted for passive voice verbs. In converting to active verbs, extraneous words are eliminated. As you did with the passive voice selection, record your reactions.

(*Informatics* is the name of the company, and "The Examiner" is the software program that processes insurance claims.)

> Informatics *formats* entry screens with field names to assist operators through each function. Operators *may enter* information in any sequence at various terminals. The Examiner *sorts* all transactions prior to the nightly batch processing cycle.
>
> Operators *may verify* daily on-line transactions and *change* or *delete* unprocessed transactions immediately.
>
> The Examiner *can furnish* a hard copy or taped report of all processed transactions after the nightly batch process. The Examiner *detects* errors during the batch process and *furnishes* an error listing report which logically *sequences* errors and identifies the terminal operator and location. The system *retains* faulty transactions, *allows* for evaluating errors: it automatically *includes* corrected transactions in the next batch cycle.

Active Voice = Economy of Language

Notice the saving in language. In the first example, the writer used 183 words; in the second example, using the active voice, the writer used 110 words, deleting more than one-third of the original writer's language. Deleting a similar percentage of words in a 10-page memorandum or a 200-page manual reduces writing time, reading-comprehension time, and dollars spent on collating, paper, and postage. More important, notice how much more easily you read the active voice selection.

Think About It

Does the fact that actors appear in the sentence decrease the efficiency with which the writer communicates his/her message?

A Gradual Move to Active

Stage 9 (Part 4) will help you to shift your writing style from passive to active. Bear in mind, your writing style shifts from passive to active voice in levels:

- Passive voice—Third Person Point of View

  The report was reviewed by me, and it stated that all trainers should take a Train the Trainer course.

- Active Voice—First Person Point of View

  I reviewed the report, which stated that all trainers should take a Train the Trainer course.

- Active Voice—Third Person Point of View

  The report stated that all trainers should take a Train the Trainer course.

Background—Passive Voice

Why Passive Is So Prevalent

Technical communicators date the modern age of technical writing to World War II when both the Allied and Axis powers manufactured staggering numbers of weapons and other products. Repair, maintenance, and operating manuals, among other documents, accompanied the hardware.

Technical writers of the World War II era took their cue from the scientific writing of the 19th century. The scientific writers favored an impersonal style in which the *subject matter* was emphasized more than the writer. The science writers described experiments in the laboratory without mentioning their own involvement in the experiments.

Passive Persists

Unfortunately, this same passive-voice oriented prose persists today. Even textbook authors who espouse the use of the active voice illustrate their books with reports written in the passive voice. Deborah Andrews and Margaret Bickle in *Technical Writing* (New York: Macmillan Publishing Company, Inc., 1982) give the following example of an acceptable report:

> . . . This plan will outline in detail how all hazardous wastes *will be handled* at the refinery . . . This application *will be forwarded* to the Legal Department for review by November 1 and then *will be submitted* to the EPA on November 19 to meet RCRA compliance requirements.
>
> [pp. 252–253]
>
> [italics mine]

To compound the stylistic infractions, the same authors, while advocating use of the active voice, *themselves* use the passive.

> A proposal is an offer to work, to do something. Such action *should be conveyed* in positive, active verbs. Don't slide back into saying what "is to be done" but describe what you (and name the people) will do.
>
> [pp. 252–253]
>
> [italics mine]

Active Voice—A Call to Clarity

Modern-day authors may resist using the active voice. History is on their side. But the active voice saves time and money.

In addition, given the growing popularity and constraints of the cathode ray tube, authors need to compose documents that are succinct. When authors present information to a computer operator within the bounds of an action screen, writers must express themselves as crisply as possible.

Think About It

Should we continue the tradition of using passive voice in technical writing simply for tradition's sake?

Are there other reasons to use passive voice?

What Is Passive Voice?

Identifying Passive Voice

There is often confusion about what constitutes passive voice. Even though we have seen some examples, we may not always recognize passive voice unless we know its characteristics. Primarily, you can identify passive voice by three characteristics:

1. The subject is acted on.
2. The predicate, or complete verb, usually contains an auxiliary, or helping, verb that is a form of the verb *to be*, (*is, are, was, be*, etc.).
3. A prepositional phrase (by someone or something) is located in the sentence.

Characteristic 1: Subject Acted On

Passive Subjects Don't Act

The first characteristic of the passive voice is that, in a passive voice sentence, the subject of the sentence is acted on. In the sentences below

> I wrote the report.
> I will write the report.

the subject ("I") acts and, therefore, is the *true subject.* In the following sentences

> The report was written by me.
> The report will be written by me.

"report" is the subject. Since report does not act, it is the *false subject,* and the verbs are in the passive voice.

> Stop reading here. Work through Exercise 13-1 to learn more about "true" and "false" subjects.

**EXERCISE 13-1
(Individual)**

Find the subject. Underline it with *one line* if it is a true subject (the subject acts) and with *two lines* if it is a false subject (the subject does not act).

1. Researchers will conduct pH, sulfates, and metals analysis in accordance with methods listed in "Methods for Chemical Analysis of Water and Wastes."
2. The standards safety committee subjected recent air quality regulation announcements to a review.
3. Recent air quality regulation announcements have been subjected to a review by the plant safety standards committee.
4. The serial multiplexer will be used to serially read the 60 or 120 groups of eight TDI detectors.
5. The CIM array is configured as 480 TDI elements arranged for oversampling in the cross scan direction.

**Characteristic 2:
Use of Auxiliary Verbs**

Helping Verbs Indicate Passive Construction

Use of auxiliary verbs, or helping verbs, that are forms of the verb *to be* is the second characteristic that often identifies passive voice constructions. Most passive voice verbs look just like the ones in the sentences below:

> The report was written by me.
> The report will be written by me.

Notice I say *often—not always.* For example, the following sentence contains the auxiliary verb "will," plus the main verb "write."

> I will write the report.

Notice two things: 1) *Will* is not a form of the verb *to be* and so that helping verb does not fit the description of the passive voice. 2) Because the subject of the above sentence acts, the predicate is not in the passive voice, but, rather, in the active voice.

Some Exceptions to the Rule

Though auxiliary verbs are usually characteristic of passive voice, the passive voice *may* not display an auxiliary verb at all. Look at the following sentence:

The report, found by the engineer, described the computer's keyboard.

In this sentence, "found" is a passive voice verb because "which," the elliptical subject of "found," does not act. The full sentence would read

The report, which was found by the engineer, described the computer's keyboard.

Stop reading here and work through Exercise 13-2 to see more about how writers use auxiliary verbs in passive voice

---

EXERCISE 13-2 (Individual)

Underline the auxiliary verb with *one line* and the main verb with *two lines* in these active and passive voice sentences.

1. Sulfates, pH, and metals analysis will be conducted in accordance with methods listed in "Methods for Chemical Analysis of Water and Wastes."
2. Researchers will conduct pH, sulfates, and metals analysis in accordance with methods listed in "Methods for Chemical Analysis of Water and Wastes."
3. The standards safety committee subjected recent air quality regulation announcements to a review.
4. The charge transfer detector is proposed for the MWIR band because it offers high sensitivity, better scan efficiency, good MTF, and no significant increase in overall risk.
5. Two transfer options will be studied during Phase 1—the charge coupled device (CCD) and the charge imaging matrix (CIM).

Characteristic 3: Agency Phrases

"By Me" Phrases

The third characteristic of passive voice is the use of "agency" prepositional phrases. In the following sentences, you notice the prepositional phrase "by me."

The report was written by me.
The report will be written by me.

The prepositional phrase "by me" or "by someone" or "by something" characterizes the passive voice.

You won't always find such a phrase following a passive voice verb. If such a phrase is not stated, then it is understood, as in the following sentence:

> The gasoline was filtered before being sent to the refinery.

The above sentence actually contains two understood phrases:

> "The gasoline was filtered [by technicians] before being sent to the refinery [by the company]."

Results of Using Passive Voice

Two Problems with Passive

When we use the passive voice, two undesirable results are possible:

- Longer sentences, because verbs are poorly focused
- Increased difficulty of comprehension for the audience.

Each result interferes with the primary goal—to communicate the message to the audience.

More Words, Less Clarity

Sometimes, when editing the passive voice, you may discover a verb that only marginally expresses the action of the sentence. For instance, the following passive voice verb fuzzily conveys the meaning of the sentence:

> This application *is used* to report employee clockings that *are gathered* from the monitoring system.
>
> (15 words)

The verb "used" glues the subject, "application," to the infinitive, "to report." However, "used" conveys little meaning; it doesn't describe what "this application" does.

Even when we convert the passive voice verb to an active voice one, employing *use*, the conversion does not enhance the meaning of the sentence:

The operator uses this application to report employee clockings that the monitoring system gathers.

The following sentence does enhance meaning and uses fewer words by employing a more sharply focused active verb:

This application *reports* employee clockings that the monitoring system records.

(10 words)

"Reports" describes what the application does, and "records" tells what the monitoring system does. By converting both passive voice verbs, you reduce the weight of the sentence by 33 percent. Again, this one-sentence saving seems insignificant by itself, but when you multiply a one-sentence saving over a 10-page report or a 200-page manual, you quickly appreciate the impact of one simple style revision—changing passive voice verbs to active voice.

Specifying the Actor

One note here with regard to converting the passive voice to the active voice—sometimes the original passive voice sentence will lack an expressed actor, as in the following sentence:

Sulfates, pH, and metals analysis *will be conducted* in accordance with methods listed in "Methods for Chemical Analysis of Water and Wastes."

In this case, you may insert "we" or "researchers" or some such reasonable actor:

We will analyze pH, sulfates, and metals according to "Methods for Chemical Analysis of Water and Wastes."

or

The project team will analyze . . .

Delayed Meaning and Decreased Comprehension

Using the passive voice makes reading more difficult because it delays the meaning of the sentence. Look at the following sentence:

The serial multiplexer will be used to serially read the 60 or 120 groups of eight TDI detectors.

Notice that the passive voice delays stating the key verb *read* until late in the sentence. To move more of the meaning to the front of the sentence, convert the passive voice to active voice so that the sentence reads:

The serial multiplexer reads the 60 or 120 groups of eight TDI detectors.

Notice, too, that I deleted "serially," a redundant word. We will discuss redundancy in the "Keeping Text Concise" segment of Stage 9 (Chapter 16).

> Stop reading here and work through Exercises 13-3, 13-4, and 13-5 to practice using sharply focused verbs to increase the clarity of your sentences.

EXERCISE 13-3 (Individual)

Revise the following sentences, replacing the poorly focused main verb with one that brings the meaning of the sentence into sharp focus.

1. The figures have been re-analyzed by our research assistants to determine the coefficient of error. The results will be announced by the principal researcher when the situation is judged appropriate.
2. These technical directives are written in a style of maximum simplicity as a result of an attempt at more effective communication with employees who have had relatively little education.
3. Recent air quality regulation announcements have been subjected to a review by the plant safety standards committee.
4. Commercial support equipment will be supported with commercial data supplied with the commercial equipment when it is purchased.
5. Nights, Saturdays, and Sundays will be utilized as required for maintenance, inspections, and preparation of the aircraft for early flight operations Monday through Friday.

EXERCISE 13-4
(Individual)

Underline all passive voice verbs in the following passage.

PROPOSED APPROACH AND PERFORMANCE

MWIR SPECTRAL BAND

The charge transfer detector is proposed for the MWIR band because it offers high sensitivity, better scan efficiency, good MTF and no significant increase in overall risk. Two transfer options will be studied during Phase 1, the charge coupled device (CCD) and the charge imaging matrix (CIM). The CCD will be considered the baseline approach because it can more readily achieve BLIP detection, requires but a simple processor chip and offers pixel aggregation as an operational tradeoff. The CIM is the secondary option offering more defect tolerance at somewhat reduced sensitivity.

CCD Array:

The proposed CCD focal plane MWIR submodule is illustrated in Figure SB4. The HgCdTe CCD detector array consists of 480 of 960 TDI detectors having essentially a 100% fill factor. Each TDI detector is a CCD shift register consisting of 8 stages with four phase gates for each stage. The four phase TDI array requires only 4 drive lines. The selection of 480 or 960 TDI detectors will be determined during the study and will depend on the cross scan MTF requirement. The serial multiplexer will be used to serially read the 60 or 120 groups of 8 TDI detectors. Thus this architecture multiplexes only 64:1 in the detector chip, a modest number compared with the 1024:1 demonstrated by Texas Instruments in 1984 under contract N00014-82-C-2409.

The basic CCD structure will be fabricated on p-type LPE HgCdTe using anodic sulfide passivation. ZnS insulator films and thin nickel films for IR transmission. Boron implant diodes will be fabricated for the output nodes. Aluminum metal films will be used for the bus lines. The active area will be highly transparent for high sensitivity and low optical

---

signature. The CCD serial multiplexer output diodes will be connected to a silicon chip by expanded metal film. The silicon chip will perform low noise buffer amplification, correlated double sampling and have all the necessary logic to drive the CCD detector chip. The silicon JC may also perform high speed multiplexing to reduce the output lead count to less than 15.

CIM Array:

The CIM array is configured as 480 TDI elements arranged for oversampling in the cross scan direction. The number of TDI may be varied but is shown as 4 in Figure SB5 to keep the scan efficiency above 70%. The detector arrangement would be similar as to that shown in Figure SB2. The 4 TDI detectors are multiplexed to one read diode for a total of 480 outputs. The fill factor is approximately 60%. The fabrication process is similar to the CCD process with the use of anodic sulfide passivation. ZnS insulator films and thin Ni detector gates. This array is also made on p-type LPE HgCdTe. The fabrication yield is higher for the CIM than the CCD because the detectors are independently coupled to the read node. However there are more required processor functions.

The CIM is coupled to the silicon processor chip by expanded metal film to produce a relatively compact structure. The silicon processor chip performs low noise buffer amplification, correlated double sampling, TDI, pixel accumulate (for enhanced dynamic range), multiplexing and provides all the necessary logic to drive the CIM.

EXERCISE 13-5 (Individual)

Refer to Exercise 12-1.

Circle all passive voice constructions in the two "write as you speak" sections of your Writing Sample.

Don't Be Passive

Say It with Active Verbs

Use the active voice as often as possible. Let it become a habit. If you don't, you will slip back into using passive voice the majority of the time.

Think About It

- How will your superiors respond to your new, "active" writing style?
- How long will it take to internalize your new, "active" style?
- Will the time come when you can write actively at the front end, or will you only revise passive voice constructions in the edit phase?

14 ···

Strengthening Verbs

CONTENTS

Lifting the Fog

"Easy" Verbs Don't Communicate

We're lazy sometimes and take the closest verb off the shelf, usually some form of the verb *to be* (is, are, been, etc.). These weak verbs force us to bulk up our sentence with extra words because the weak verb communicates only a hazy meaning to the audience. Strong verbs focus meaning quickly and eliminate the need for supporting words.

"To Be" Doesn't "Make" It

We stuff information into ponderous nouns and expect weak verbs like forms of the verb "to be" to carry the meaning of our sentences:

> The determination of cross-section is dependent on the transmitted frequency. With lower-frequency, wavelengths are bigger, and angular resolution (beamwidth) is larger.

We expect verbs like "make" to convey meaning to our audiences:

> In the past several years, the STL has made several key sensor exploitation technological developments.

Strong Verbs Communicate Clearly

Instead, create clearer messages with strong verbs:

> Determining cross-section depends on the transmitted frequency. With lower frequency, wavelengths increase (in size), and angular resolution (beamwidth) increases, too.

> In the past several years, the STL has developed several key sensor exploitation technologies.

What You Will Learn

In this chapter, you will learn to

1. Recognize weak verbs.
2. Convert weak verbs to strong verbs.
3. Recognize expletive-plus-weak-verb constructions.
4. Convert expletives and weak verbs to true subjects and strong verbs.
5. Identify nominals.
6. Convert nominals to strong verbs.

Why Strong Verbs?

Strong Verbs Vs. Weak Verbs

Strong verbs like *weld, singe, salivate, bulldoze,* and *inject* create images. On the other hand, weak verbs like *is, was,* and other forms of the verb *to be,* and *do, make, provide,* and *include* say little, if anything. These weak verbs cause audiences to spend more time *deciphering* meaning rather than *reading it.*

Look at an Example

Note the difference in the same sentence with two different verbs:

> The Covert Penetration Processor (CPP) *has* the digital map database, including known threat information.

vs.

> The Covert Penetration Processor (CPP) *stores* the digital map database, including known threat information.

The Advantages of Strong Verbs

Use of the strongest possible verbs enables audiences to comprehend meaning quickly. For instance, look at the following sentence:

> The shopowner *fastened* the steel bar to the steel pipe.

The audience directly understands that someone has joined two pieces of metal. However, if you revise the verb to read,

> The shopowner *welded* the steel bar to the steel pipe.

you create an even more "visual" sense of joining *and* color—that of a man dressed in a protective apron and hood, lighted acetylene torch in hand, gaze riveted on two pieces of metal he attempts to weld.

The more appropriate verb, *welded*, improves the sentence and also infuses surrounding sentences with greater color and meaning. And when meaning is clear, the audience can read with greater comprehension and speed.

Strong Verbs in Poetry

A poem, "About Motion Pictures," by an unknown author, captures the power of verbs:

> "Get the verb right
>   and directing is a cinch,"
> he said modestly, gesturing
> toward his newest masterpiece.
>
> The same is said for poetry.
> Strike adjectives, adverbs!
> Red-pencil ands and buts.
> Get the verb right
>   and writing is a cinch.
>
> It's true in living.
>   Move. Scintillate.
>   Grasp. Dodge.
>   Placate.
>   Grow.
> Get the verb right
>   and living is a cinch.
>
> The verb is get.

Strong Verbs in Technical Passages

Now let's apply the power of strong verbs in poetry to technical documents. Read the following illustration, laced with weak verbs:

> ***Equivalent Circuit, Output High.*** Figure 7 *is* an illustration of the standard TTL gate input-low, output-high state. At least one of the inputs *is* low. Usually, the input to this gate *is* the output of a preceding TTL gate. With input voltage low, the base-emitter PN junction for this particular Q1 input is forward biased. Transistor Q1 *has* stray capacitance and drops the Q2 base voltage. Q2 and Q4 are cutoff. Q2 and Q4 bases are never back-biased, but the voltage drops below the conduction "knee" for both base-emitter junctions.

Now examine the reworked version of the previous passage, this time with strong verbs:

> ***Equivalent Circuit, Output High.*** Figure 7 *illustrates* the standard TTL gate input-low, output-high state. At least one of the inputs is low. Usually, the output of a preceding TTL *drives* this "low" input. With input voltage low, the system forward biases the base emitter PN junction for this particular Q1 input. Transistor Q1 *stores* stray charge and drops the Q2 base voltage. The system cuts off Q2 and Q4. The system never back-biases the Q2 and Q4 bases, but the voltage drops below the conduction "knee" for both base emitter junctions.

Another Technical Example

Examine the following passage in which the author uses weak verbs:

> Goals *include* evolutionary upgrades in capability of existing systems and revolutionary advances in capability for new systems while *providing* increased reliability and maintainability, improved performance, and lower life-cycle costs.

I have rewritten the passage, using strong verbs:

> Goals:
>
> - *Upgrade* capability of existing systems
> - *Revolutionize* the capability of new systems
> - *Increase* reliability and maintainability
> - *Improve* performance
> - *Lower* life-cycle costs.

> Stop reading now and work through Exercise 14-1 to practice changing weak verbs to strong ones.

EXERCISE 14-1 (Individual)

Change the weak verbs to strong verbs in the following sentences.

1. The research findings are indicative of the fact that heavy air pollution may cause cancer.
2. The XYZ Corporation held out to the end against the attacks of its competitor.
3. Roberta acquired an advantage early on by learning COBOL.
4. A compiler is a program that takes the programmer's instructions and translates them into instructions the computer can understand.
5. This brief discussion of generic TTL gates provides an explanation of how basic digital circuits function.

Weak Verbs and Expletives

Expletives Often Accompany Weak Verbs

You continually see, "There is," "There are," "Here is," and "Here are" in manuscripts. *There* and *here* are expletives. Authors may also use *It*, plus a form of the verb *to be*, as an expletive plus weak verb. Authors tend to begin sentences with these crutch words because many authors don't expend the effort necessary to sort out the true subject and place it first.

For instance, look at the following sentence:

There will be one line for each column to be printed on the report.

"There" is not the true subject of the sentence. "There" is the false subject of the sentence; it stands in the spot, structurally, where the subject normally appears. The true subject of the sentence is "column." The sentence should read:

Each column appears in one line of the report.

Hint—Find the True Subject

Find the true subject in a sentence that begins with an expletive and a weak verb, and place the true subject at the front of the sentence; then follow the true subject with a strong verb.

Remember, audiences will most easily process words arranged in subject-verb-object word order. Make sure your sentences march along in this basic order.

> Stop reading now and work through Exercise 14-2 to practice removing expletives and rewriting sentences with strong verbs.

EXERCISE 14-2 (Individual)

First, underline with *one line* the expletive and weak verb in each of the following sentences. Then, underline with *two lines* the true subject. Finally, revise the sentence, placing the true subject first in the sentence and supplying a strong verb to accompany the true subject.

1. There are many Daisy-DNIX commands, but you can be productive with a relatively small subset, listed below.

2. The fact that there were impure chemicals caused the delay.

3. If there is not enough room to list all the desired fields on one line, put a comma after the last one of the first line, then continue on the next line by keying-in an "F" and completing the list of desired field codes.

4. There were at least a hundred chemicals that were added to the list.

5. It was recognized that if a resonance should occur, large losses would be introduced in the range of the resonant frequency and that from a practical viewpoint the transformer could not be used in such a region.

Nominals

Prefer Strong Verbs to Nominals

Nominals, or nominalizations, are verbs that have been converted to nouns. Many of these nouns would have been better left verbs.

Examples of Nominals

Examine the following sentences:

> The engineers and the programmers brought the project to a *conclusion*.
>
> The judge took into *consideration* the facts of the case.
>
> The pollsters were of the *opinion* that Governor Dewey would win over incumbent President Truman.
>
> The lab assistants carried out the *experiments* with the dogfish while the instructors delivered the *lectures*.
>
> The advertising executives are found to be in *agreement* on the design for the company logo.

Removing the Nominals

Are the above sentences constructed as tightly as possible? Substitute the following sentences for the ones above:

> The engineers and programmers concluded the project.
>
> The judge considered the facts of the case.
>
> The pollsters believed that Governor Dewey would defeat incumbent President Truman.
>
> The lab assistants experimented with the dogfish while the instructors lectured.
>
> The advertising executives agreed on the design for the company's logo.

In all cases, we saved language and more precisely stated the meaning of the sentences.

Hint—Recognizing Nominals

You may have noticed that four of the five nominals in the first set of sentences—"consideration," "opinion," "experiment," and "agreement"—end in -ion or -ment. Nominals don't always have one of these two endings (see "lecture"), but these two suffixes often indicate that you may have a nominal in your writing. I say often because not every noun with an -ion or -ment suffix is a nominal that needs to be converted to a verb. For instance, look at the following sentence:

> The court weighed the consideration the buyer paid for the merchandise.

In this sentence, "consideration," a legal term, must remain intact. If we tried to work "considered" into the sentence, we would distort the meaning.

Let's look at another example:

> The reduction of taxes was a major promise of the present administration.

In this sentence, "reduction" and "promise" are nominals and "administration" is not. The revised sentence should read

> The present administration promised to reduce taxes.

Stop reading now and work through Exercises 14-3 and 14-4 to practice recognizing and reworking nominals.

EXERCISE 14-3 (Individual)

First, underline all of the nominals in the following sentences. Then edit the sentences, converting the nominals to strong verbs.

1. The voltage regulator was put to a severe test before being installed.
2. The computer responds with a reply.
3. The rapid shrinkage of the foam away from the flame results in a failure of this test to make reliable discriminations among certain materials.
4. Ceramics have excellent heat retention and wear resistance.

**EXERCISE 14-4
(Individual)**

Refer to Exercise 12-1.

Identify weak verbs (expletives plus weak verbs and nominals, too) in the "write as you speak" draft of your Writing Sample by boxing them.

Muscle Up Your Prose

Use Strong Verbs

Does meaning "spring off the page" of your documents? If not, examine the verbs you are using. Are you using strong, active verbs that vividly convey meaning? Or are you cluttering your writing with weak verbs (*is, was, provide, include*), expletives, and nominals that obscure your message?

Use strong verbs—and see the benefits in your writing.

15 ·

Eliminating Jargon

CONTENTS

Some Call It Gobbledegook

A Different Language

Users complain about the unnecessary specialized vocabulary experts use in reports. Various audiences complain about the "bureaucratese," "spec-ese," or inflated language that report writers use in an attempt to sound professional.

Writers should use the more easily understood word, no matter who the audience is. *A reader will never return a report and say, "I'm sorry. The words you used were too simple, and the report was too easy for me to understand."*

What You Will Learn

In this chapter, you will learn to

1. Identify jargon more readily.
2. Substitute more easily understood words for unnecessary jargon.
3. Verify that your audience understands the acronyms you use.
4. Avoid neologisms (new words).

A Call for Simplicity

A Formula for Simplicity

Clear, simple writing need not be difficult. You can take a giant step toward clarity by monitoring use of the following in your documents:

- Jargon
- Euphemisms
- Acronyms
- Neologisms (new words).

Jargon

Use the More Easily Understood Word

We have been conditioned to prefer longer, more complicated words over simple words. We "sound" more professional when we encourage complexity rather than simplicity. Listeners and readers tend to equate simplicity with simplistic.

Nothing could be further from the truth. Physicists refer to the simplest solution as the most "elegant" one.

Complexity Obscures Meaning

Look at the following "technical" passage. What does it mean?

> The following describes the activities of five immature mammals of the family of nonruminant artiodactyl ungulates. All five of these may be described as being of less than average magnitude; however, no information is given as to the relative size of one with respect to another. Available evidence indicates that the first of the group proceeded in the direction of an area previously established for the purpose of commerce. Data on the second of the group clearly show that, at least during the time period under consideration, it remained within the confines of its own place of residence. Reports received on the activities of the third member of the group seem to show conclusively that it possessed an unknown quantity of the flesh of a bovine animal, prepared for consumption by exposure to dry heat. The only information available on the fourth member of the group is of a wholly negative nature, namely, that its possessions did not include any material of the type previously described as having been in the possession of its predecessor in this discussion. As to the fifth and last member of the group, fairly conclusive evidence points to its having made, during the entire course of a movement in the direction of its place of residence, a noise described as "wee, wee, wee."

When you arrived at the last line of the passage, you discovered that you were reading a "technical" description of "This Little Piggy Went to Market!" No doubt, the last line conjured pleasant childhood images of your smiling mother or father counting your toes and reciting the rhyme. However, you were probably annoyed at the work it took for you to extract the meaning from this child's story.

An Inappropriate Approach

The story was obscured by scientific (biological) jargon—*immature mammals, nonruminant artiodactyl ungulates*—and by euphemisms. (I will discuss euphemisms in the next section.) Biological jargon may be appropriate for some audiences, but certainly not for the audience for this nursery rhyme.

Defining Jargon

Jargon is specialized vocabulary used by professionals in medicine, law, science, technology, music, and other fields. Examples of jargon are *myocardial infarction, habeas corpus, astral, bit, allegro. Myocardial infarction* may be necessary jargon for a doctor to indicate a particular kind of heart attack. Use of jargon depends on the intent of the author and the ability of the audience to understand the specialized language.

The Price of Jargon

Unfortunately, too many audiences complain that experts (engineers, computer scientists, for example) use too much jargon in documents meant for less well informed audiences. Technicians complain that engineers clutter manuals with unnecessary theory, and hardware and software users complain that computer manuals are incomprehensible because of too much jargon.

Can You Decipher This?

What would you do if confronted by the following description?

> AutoCAD does not actually draw a displacement line, it gets the information it needs from the displacement points. If you are picking displacement points on the screen, AutoCAD will show you a temporary displacement line trailing behind the crosshair from the first point you pick until you pick the second. You can see how this works by looking at MOVE DISPLACEMENT.

A Better Way

One engineer solved the problem this way:

> There are many ways to move an object using AutoCAD. Any time you move an object, there are two reference points needed. The first point is a reference of the start point or base point. The second is the location where you want the object to end up or its displacement.

The engineer revised the passage by stating the purpose of the description in the first sentence. He also deleted the jargon *displacement line* and *displacement points* and supplied an implied definition of *displacement* in the last line.

The Best Way

A second engineer supplied the best solution by honing the purpose statement (the first sentence) with an even sharper edge and by supplying two clear, informal definitions:

> When you move an object using AutoCAD, note two reference points: the starting, or base, point; and the ending, or displacement, point.

More Examples of Jargon

In an attempt to sound more "professional," we manufacture expressions—usually longer expressions—which stretch our messages. Even though we have already created "vocabularies" which certain groups of experts employ, two questions arise:

- Should we have created these vocabularies?
- Having done this, should we compound the problem by adding to these "accepted" vocabularies?

Consider the following example:

> Producibility is defined as an improved way to build. This is not a change which makes a nonproducible part producible. Such a change should be classified as performance. Producibility can be a cost, time, process, or material savings.

We can improve this jargon-filled statement by changing the point of view and converting passive voice constructions to active voice ones:

> Let's define *producibility* as an improved way to build. This definition excludes changes to fix nonproducible parts; we would classify such nonproducible changes as *performance*. A producibility ECN saves cost, time, and materials and improves the building process.

We can improve the original statement even more by beginning this way:

> A producibility ECN is defined as a change that saves . . .

Other examples:

> The soldier dug his foxhole with a combat entrenching tool.

What's a combat entrenching tool? A shovel! Some instructional designers speak of *informational displays* rather than *definitions* and *examples*.

> Stop reading now and work through Exercise 15-1 to practice identifying and eliminating jargon.

EXERCISE 15-1 (Individual)

Rewrite the following words and phrases, substituting more easily understood language for jargon.

1. glitch

2. debug

3. sanitation engineer

4. utilize

5. ingress

6. egress

7. The determination of cross-section is dependent on the
transmitted frequency.

8. I will discuss how helical wrap construction increases detection capabilities.

9. However, in addition, interaction with the customer and other audiences serves to impress the customer with the quality of both the simulation and the system.

10. Risk analysis evaluates a company's ability to produce a product that can perform its defined mission objectives.

Euphemisms

What Are Euphemisms?

Euphemisms are high-flown, longer words that authors substitute for harsher sounding, usually shorter words. Euphemisms cushion the blow of unpleasant occurrences. When someone in the family dies, we say that the family member "passed away" or is "deceased." We shy away from saying the person "died." In referring to someone's stature, we might say that she is "petite" or that he is "diminutive" rather than "short." We all remember the nursery rhyme, "Little Jack Horner." Look at the same lines dressed up in euphemistic language:

> Diminutive Jack Horner reclined in a mural intersection, masticating yuletide pastry. He inserted his polar dexter and extracted a delectable fruit and exclaimed: "Oh! How I am prodigiously precocious."

Euphemisms Hide Your Meaning

Euphemisms sound lovely and important, but they have no place in clear documents. They clutter documents because of their size, and they obscure meaning because they are not easily understood by most audiences. Euphemistic language can even cloud the following message, which we would recognize quickly if expressed in less ornate language:

> The probability of striking the ground, including ground-based obstacles, increases greatly with the onset of inclement weather.

Why couldn't the author who wrote that memo have said, instead,

> Chances of hitting the ground, or any obstacle on the ground, increase with bad weather.

> Stop reading now and work through Exercises 15-2 to practice simplifying your writing.

**EXERCISE 15-2
(Individual)**

Rewrite the following "old saws" in their original language. I'll do a few for you.

1. Scintillate, scintillate, astra minific.

   Twinkle, twinkle, little star.

2. Surveillance should precede saltation.

3. It is fruitless to become lachrymose over precipitately decanted lacteal fluid.

   Don't cry over spilled milk.

4. Eschew the implement of correction and vitiate the scion.

5. Sorting on the part of mendicants must be extirpated.

6. Eleemosynary deeds originate intramurally.

   Charity begins at home.

7. Circumspection requires that individuals abiding in vitreous edifices refrain from launching petrous projectiles.

8. Neophytic serendipity.

   Beginner's luck.

9. The person presenting the ultimate cachination possesses thereby the optimal cachination.

10. Abstention from uncertain undertakings precludes a potential escalation of remuneration.

11. Missiles of ligneous or oterous consistency have the potential of fracturing my osseous structure, but vocalized appellations will eternally remain innocuous.

12. It is fruitless to attempt to indoctrinate a superannuated canine with innovative maneuvers.

13. Freedom from grimy encrustation is contiguous to rectitude.

    Cleanliness is next to Godliness.

14. All articles that coruscate with resplendence are not truly auriferous.

15. Where there are visible emissions from combustible materials, there is conflagration.

16. Male cadavers are incapable of yielding testimony.

17. Members of avian species of identical plumage congregate.

18. The stylus is more potent that the rapier.

19. A revolving lithic conglomeration accumulates no congeries of small bryophytic herbage.

20. The temperature of the aqueous content of an unremittingly ogled vessel will never reach 212 degrees Fahrenheit.

Acronyms

Acronyms in Technical Communication

More and more acronyms find their way into conversations and meetings and into subsequent technical documents. These shortened forms of verbal and written communication are understood by many, some, or none, depending on the audience's familiarity with the subject. Many acronyms are words in that they can be pronounced. RAM (random-access memory) and ROM (read-only memory) are examples of acronyms used by computer scientists. Notice that acronyms do not contain periods and that all letters are capitalized.

A Recipe for Alphabet Soup

Acronyms can pollute documents in the same ways that jargon, inflated language, and euphemisms may. The following passage illustrates this:

> Specific QRA policies and procedures for the DSEG are issued in the DSEG QSPs by the Group QRA manager. Procedures in the QSPs are applicable to all DSEG functions and organizations. Supplementary QRA procedures shall be issued by division and site QRA functions to ensure compliance with DSEG quality system procedures.

Consider the Audience

Instead of clarifying information, acronyms may confuse unknowing readers. Verify that your reader understands the acronyms you use, or create a glossary to define your acronyms. Also, do not use so many unfamiliar acronyms that your audience must continually page between the glossary and text.

Be careful with acronyms, but don't avoid them. Proper use of acronyms can save time for both you and your audience.

Refer to Chapter 17, "Writing Professional Documents," for a discussion of rules covering the use of acronyms in technical documents.

Neologisms

What Are Neologisms?

"Arrogant" authors tend to create new words; however, these newly created words—understood only by the author or a few others—confound most audiences. These newly created words, or neologisms, confuse audiences unready for variations of words they have seen before.

No Such Word

For example, we have the verb *perturbed*: "That solution to the problem perturbed me." We also have the noun *perturbation*:

"She suffered the many perturbations associated with studying for the electrical engineering degree." But we do not yet have the neologism *perturbate*, as in "That solution to the problem perturbated me."

More Examples

Look at the following example from the technical realm:

> Receiver thermal noise *perturbs* the incoming signal. Major *perturbations* of the input produce large variations in the output. We will *perturbate* the sequence of data samples to ensure statistical independence.

Perturbate is a neologism.

Apply the same thinking to *console, consolation,* and *consolate*. There is no such animal as *consolate*.

A colleague spotted this neologism in a computer manual:

> . . . will issue an *informatory* message on the screen.

Informatory, a neologism that would have stopped me in my tracks, is supposed to distinguish between messages that inform and those that don't.

Words like *informatory* only confuse audiences. Avoid deriving unaccepted words from known words.

> Stop reading now and work through Exercise 15-3 to practice finding jargon, euphemisms, acronyms, and neologisms.

EXERCISE 15-3 (Individual)

Refer to Exercise 12-1.

Underline all examples of jargon, euphemisms, confusing acronyms, and neologisms in the two "Write as You Speak" sections of your Writing Sample.

Write to Express—Not Impress

Keep It Simple

Use the simple word whenever possible even with sophisticated audiences. Even the experts will thank you for making life easier for them. Use jargon only when necessary and not to appear more "professional." Write to express, not to impress. Avoid euphemisms, excessive use of acronyms, and neologisms to make sure your writing is as clear as possible.

16 ·······························

Keeping Text Concise

CONTENTS

So Many Words, So Little Content

Content Words Communicate Your Ideas

The English language contains content words and structure words. The content words, like *Texas Instruments, Park Central VI, John Jones*, and *sensor*, account for 600,000 words—approximately 70 percent of the language. The structure words, like *in, but, for, who, is*, and *therefore*, account for approximately 30 percent of the language. Yet, when we write, we reverse the percentages and use 70 percent structure words and 30 pecent content words. We should strive to regain the balance of 70 percent to 30 pecent in favor of content words. The techniques you will learn in addressing this problem will help you avoid the use of unnecessary structure words that clutter your message.

What You Will Learn

In this chapter, you will learn to

1. Identify and eliminate redundancies.
2. Eliminate unnecessary relative pronouns.
3. Eliminate unnecessary auxiliary verbs.

The Art of Wordsmithing

Trim the Fat

"Wordsmith" your documents carefully. Wordsmithing means taking the time to edit your documents carefully, selecting the proper words and paring away unnecessary language. Wordsmithing is trimming the fat, being concise, choosing only significant facts to include in your documents.

Delete whenever you can. Cut away the fat to expose the muscle:

- Delete unnecessary words
- Delete insignificant facts—even if they are expressed concisely.

Delete Unnecessary Words

We're lazy, and we're also slaves to habit. To relate that to this section, let me first say that we take words off the shelf—sometimes any word that's handy. We don't think about our actions—we just reach up to the shelf and say, "This looks like a good one. It fits the situation, kind of." Second, we see others—those in authority—write expressions, and we use the same ones. It's the old peer pressure game. Unnecessary words hinder our ability to communicate, but because someone "safe" (someone in an approved position) uses them, we follow.

Choose your words carefully. Be sensitive to situations in which unnecessary words may occur. Be a wordsmith. At first, wordsmithing will "eat your time." But good habits are formed just as easily as bad habits, and soon you will find yourself ferreting out unnecessary words in all your writing.

Emphasize Content Words

Remember to concentrate on content words—don't write documents that are overburdened with structure words. Infuse documents with as many content words as possible, and use structure words only when necessary to glue content together.

Redundant Words

Repetition Vs. Redundancy

Repeating words and phrases judiciously throughout a technical document can prove an informative and persuasive strategy. For example, when proposal writers repeat their company's name or reiterate key product benefits, they help persuade the audience that their company can do the job. Repeating product features and benefits throughout an advertisement helps the audience remember key information and ideas. However, do not confuse judicious repetition with *redundancy*, that is, stated or implied repetition with no purpose.

Looking for Redundancy

Different kinds of redundancy add length to sentences without adding meaning. Identify the different kinds of redundancy and then eliminate them from your manuscripts.

Search your technical manuscript for the following types of redundancy.

Intensifiers—Superfluous Adverbs

Example:

The system exhibited very powerful data management capabilities.

Example:

She reported that the project was absolutely complete.

In both examples, the adverbs add nothing to the meaning of the sentences. In fact, the sentences are stronger without the adverbs, since the sentences contain fewer words and their meaning is more readily apparent. In the second example, when a subject "completes" an action, that action is over with; "absolutely" adds nothing to the meaning of "complete." I would rewrite both sample sentences to read:

The system exhibited powerful data management capabilities.

and

She reported that the project was complete.

An author may write, "The file was completely erased." What does the author mean here? Let's examine the act of erasing. When something is erased, it is considered gone. Does the word *completely* say anything more about erasing? If the file had been "partially erased," that information would be useful, but this sentence can do well enough without "completely."

Weasel or Hedge Words

Example:

There are many Wordstar commands, but you can be productive with the relatively small subset listed below.

"Relatively" hedges the size of the subset. How many commands will allow the user to "be productive"? Either say, quantitatively, how many commands are necessary, or drop "relatively," for "relatively" tells the user nothing about "small."

An author may also try to hedge by using an auxiliary verb:

Example:

The program may execute properly if you employ these commands in the proper order.

The author covers himself/herself here by avoiding the responsibility for successful operation of the program even if the user follows directions. Edit this statement to read:

The program executes properly if you employ these commands in the proper order.

Repeating Meaning in a Different Form

Example:

She awakened at 6:00 a.m. in the morning.

Either "a.m." or "in the morning" communicates time of day.

Unneeded Emphasis

Example:

I, myself, will conduct the training session.

"I" says it all—no need to underscore my participation as leader of the training session.

Longwinded Expressions

Example:

In today's modern world, technology enhances our lives.

Example:

A large segment of the engineers agreed that organizing information was a major problem.

Save language by recasting the sentences:

Today, technology enhances our lives.

Most engineers agreed that organizing information was a major problem.

Phrases Others Use

Example:

The cold facts of the matter are . . .

Example:

It is my personal opinion . . .

Others, especially those in authority, impress us with the expressions they utter. We imitate those who impress us. Unfortunately, these authoritarian figures sometimes use incorrect, hackneyed expressions, and we perpetuate their mistakes.

> Stop reading now and work through Exercise 16-1 to practice identifying redundancies.

EXERCISE 16-1 (Individual)

Underline the redundant words in the following sentences.

1. Researchers list the resultant effects of their investigations.

2. The study was absolutely essential before the operation was begun.

3. These gritty materials, of course, contribute very significantly to the abrasive problem.

4. For the most part, the samples obtained at the lower temperatures were quite grayish colored and somewhat abrasive.

5. Each of these phases was indeed completed.

Relative Pronouns

Defining Relative Pronouns

The relative pronouns are words like *who, which,* and *that,* which introduce clauses that modify nouns and pronouns.

Can You Do Without Them?

Look at the following sentence:

The technical writer *who* produced that manual works for our company.

"Who" introduces the clause "who produced that manual." We cannot delete "who" from the sentence without the sentence losing its sense. However, consider the following sentence:

The government contractor which is located in Ohio received the contract from the Army.

In this sentence, we can delete the relative pronoun "which" and the auxiliary verb "is," and the sentence still makes sense.

The government contractor located in Ohio received the contract from the Army.

Stop reading now and work through Exercise 16-2 to practice recognizing unnecessary relative pronouns.

EXERCISE 16-2 (Individual)

Delete unnecessary relative pronouns and perform other language-saving operations.

1. Martin is a man who never misses a meeting.
2. These units have the advantage that they can be maintained or replaced after the test series has been initiated.
3. Most of these mechanisms exhibit few of the characteristics the average person would associate with the term *robot*: they are mostly machines that are capable of only the simplest kinds of motions.

Auxiliary Verbs

Definition—Auxiliary Verbs

An auxiliary verb supports a main verb. Together, the auxiliary and main verbs form the sentence's predicate.

Check the Meaning Before You Delete

Look at the following example:

Companies should create documentation much earlier in the product development cycle.

This sentence needs the auxiliary verb "should" to complete its sense: the author of the sentence exhorts companies to rethink the role of documentation "in the product development cycle." To omit "should" and say, "Companies create documentation much earlier in the product development cycle" is to misstate the sense of the sentence.

However, we can delete the auxiliary verb in the following sentence:

Do not remove your diskettes if your system should fail.

We can substitute the present tense verb "fails" for "should fail" without disturbing the conditional meaning the author intends.

Auxiliary Verbs and Tense

Mistakes in tense can also lead to the presence of extraneous auxiliary verbs. Look at the following sentence:

The technician had closed the door after leaving the lab.

In this sentence, two clauses represent two past actions. A rule of grammar states that if the action mentioned first in the sentence actually occurs second in the chronology of both events, then the author must signal this to the reader by using the past perfect tense (auxiliary verb + past participle). However, in this sentence, the action of the first mentioned event (closing the door) occurs first in the chronology of both events, and so the past perfect tense verb, "had closed" is unnecessary. The sentence should correctly read:

The technician closed the door after leaving the lab.

> Stop reading now and work through Exercises 16-3 and 16-4 to practice keeping text concise.

**EXERCISE 16-3
(Individual)**

Delete auxiliary verbs wherever possible.

1. When you have finished with Topic Six, you should take the test.
2. The manager expected the writer to have finished the report by tomorrow.
3. Engineering Support Services had produced the brochure two weeks after Marketing Services had asked for it.
4. This application will also compute regular hours worked by each employee, overtime hours that were worked and represent the actual clockings in both standard minutes and hundredths of hours. After all clockings for an employee, totals are presented by workcenter and total for the day.

**EXERCISE 16-4
(Individual)**

Refer to Exercise 12-1.

Underline with two lines all redundant words, unnecessary relative pronouns, and auxiliary verbs in the "write as you speak" draft of your Writing Sample.

Be a Wordsmith

Less Is More

Strive to write concise, clear text. Again, in order to achieve conciseness:

- Delete insignificant facts.
- Reduce jargon to simpler language.
- Eliminate redundancy.
- Watch for unnecessary use of relative pronouns and auxiliary verbs.

In addition, remember lessons about conciseness you have previously learned:

- Use active voice over passive voice.
- Prefer strong verbs to weak ones.
- Prefer strong verbs to nominals.

17 ·

Writing Professional Documents

CONTENTS

Polishing the Rough Spots

What Makes a Report Unprofessional?

Unprofessional appearing documents contain errors in grammar, usage, spelling, capitalization, and punctuation. They also fail to conform to accepted stylistic guidelines related to format, abbreviations, symbols, and proprietary names. Even though we often hear that grammatical rules are not very important, the first things readers notice in any document are errors in grammar, spelling, etc.

A Bad Impression

Make no mistake, error-filled reports reflect poorly on a company and give the impression that its approach to manufacturing products may be just as sloppy.

What You Will Learn

In this chapter, you will learn to

1. Appreciate the importance of correctness and consistency in producing professional-looking documents.
2. Identify appropriate resources to consult in order to decide questions of style, grammar, usage, mechanics, and spelling.
3. Identify 12 major errors in grammar, usage, punctuation, and capitalization and know how to correct them.

The Importance of Professionalism

The Stigma of Correctness

"The teacher emphasized mechanics so much that I tightened up and wrote stilted sentences for the rest of my life."

"I can't stand grammar!"

"As long as a document communicates, what difference does it make if all the "i's" are dotted and the "t's" are crossed?"

The first two statements seem all too true. Most students recoiled from learning the rules and "exceptions" announced in traditional grammar handbooks, for students viewed working with these handbooks as punishment for failing to write effective themes. In addition to "bleeding" all over student themes, English teachers gloried in finger pointing admonitions like, "Johnny, use *whom* instead of *who!*" And so Johnny hypercorrected for the rest of life with *whom*, even where the construction called for *who*. Johnny also tightened up so much, that when called to write, he scrawled canned, formal, "safe," accepted phrases that resulted in a patchwork, stilted style.

Grammar, usage, punctuation, capitalization, and spelling are much more than crossing "t's" and dotting "i's"; their correct use reflects the care that a company exercises in developing its documentation *and* its hardware and software products. If a company's documentation is shoddy, can its other products be any better?

Hitting the High Points

In this section, we will discuss only the major errors that plague technical communicators. This discussion will not be an encyclopedic treatment of grammar, usage, punctuation, capitalization, and spelling. You can find that kind of treatment in a grammar handbook if you feel the need to go beyond this discussion.

Consistency

What Is Consistency?

Consistency, like correctness, is crucial to the professional look of documents. However, consistency—which means doing something the same way, over and over—may mean deviating from convention, or correctness. For example, *The Chicago Manual of Style* suggests placing first-level headings in all capitals and centered. But some companies may left justify first-level headings in mixed case with underscoring. Another company may spell *center* as *centre* in order to attach an antique mood to its products.

Strive for Consistency

No matter what the company's idiosyncratic tendencies, follow them unless they are blatantly wrong and reflect poorly on the company, and follow them uniformly throughout the manuscript.

Reference Books

A Variety of Resources

No list of reference works is ever complete for writers. Good writers add to their reference shelves continually. However, you should begin with a nucleus of reference books—dictionaries, thesauruses, style manuals, grammar handbooks, rhetoric handbooks, and military standards. Since you're familiar with dictionaries and thesauruses and most likely have them on hand, I'll discuss the last four only.

Style Manuals

Types of Style Manuals

Two different types of style manuals exist:

- Traditional style manuals, published by major external publishers
- Company style manuals, compiled and published in-house.

Traditional style manuals are usually more conservative and reflect prescriptive attitudes. Company style manuals are usually more liberal in their interpretation of rules and reflect the individual needs and attitudes of particular companies.

Typical Rules in Company Manuals

Many companies produce style manuals; many do not. The following rules typify the approach some companies take in creating their own style rules:

The Acme Corporation should always be written in full—never abbreviated and never shortened in any way (e.g., Acme or Acme Corp.).

In all Acme Corporation documents, each item in a vertical list should be preceded by a bullet.

In vertical lists, the last item in the list should always be followed by a period.

All products produced by the Acme Corporation should be capitalized in normal usage—e.g., Flight Guidance System, Advanced Radar Unit, etc.

Traditional Style Manuals

Three of the best known traditional style manuals are *The Chicago Manual of Style*, *Words Into Type*, and *The Government Printing Office Style Manual*. You can purchase the first two in any major commercial or college bookstore, and the third is available from the federal government.

These style manuals, and others like them, contain generally accepted standards for formatting, grammar, usage, punctuation, capitalization, and spelling. Many different companies use *The Chicago Manual* and *Words Into Type*. In fact, most companies consider *The Chicago Manual* the bible of style manuals. Government contractors use the *Government Printing Office Style Manual* because of its authority in production of government documents, but commercial companies also use this manual as a recognized, general backup to *The Chicago Style Manual*. One failsafe approach for companies is to have all three style manuals on hand to compare solutions to knotty stylistic problems.

Examine a Typical Style Question

For instance, you may encounter the following stylistic problem: What kind of punctuation should you use for a vertical list introduced in the following way?

Users may compare computer peripherals to

    stereo components
    a carburetor
    the human brain

You are confronted with choices, and a style manual can assist you in choosing an accepted solution. First, you examine this vertical list and its introductory phrasing, wondering whether to use a colon after "to." You consult your style manual and learn that a colon is unnecessary. In another case, like the following one,

Users may compare computer peripherals to the following items:

    stereo components
    a carburetor
    the human brain

the colon is necessary.

Another Issue

Next, you wonder whether to place commas after the items in the vertical list. Most traditional style manuals stipulate that writers should treat introductory constructions and their subsequent vertical lists as complete sentences, punctuating all elements accordingly. You would then regard the items in the vertical list as items in a series, placing commas after the initial items and a period after the last item:

Users may compare computer peripherals to the following items:

> stereo components,
> a carburetor,
> the human brain.

Possible Exceptions

You might even insert an *and* after the second item, as you ordinarily would in a linear sentence. However, you may wonder whether the style manual should be controlling in all cases, including this one. For instance, you know that marketing people often use vertical lists to focus on information. Sometimes, these writers omit the commas so that readers appreciate fully the "discreteness" of each item; to further underscore the discreteness of each item, the marketing person may capitalize the initial letter of each item. Both of these practices—omitting the commas and inserting initial capitals—violate traditional thinking. What do you do? You may wish to omit commas and/or the initial capitals in this vertical list, depending on the purpose of the document.

And Another Thing . . .

You may want to consider another punctuation issue with regard to vertical lists. If you want to call even greater attention to the items in a list, you may place bullets, dashes, or numbers in front of the items. Your style manual probably will not address this issue, and so you must decide, based on audience, company convention, or personal preference.

Grammar Handbooks

What Grammar Handbooks Cover

Grammar handbooks overlap with traditional style manuals in that both address punctuation, capitalization, usage, and spelling.

However, style manuals usually do not resolve grammar and syntax problems—these problems are the province of grammar handbooks. Grammar, for example, deals with proper use of nominative and objective case, correct inflection of verb forms, agreement of subject and verb, and agreement of pronoun and antecedent. Syntax deals with proper word order—the arrangement of words in sentences so that sentences are most clearly understood.

Using a Grammar Handbook

When you have a problem in determining the correct verb for the following sentence, you should consult a grammar handbook—not a style manual:

> Neither the engineer or the technical writers (wants, want) to write this particular manual.

The grammar handbook will show that *want* is correct because the verb should agree with that part of the compound subject closer to the verb.

Your "ear" will also suggest to you that the sentence contains a conjunction problem. The grammar handbook will show that *neither* and *nor* are coordinating conjunctions and should be used as a pair. The sentence should correctly read:

> Neither the engineer nor the technical writers want to write this particular manual.

Another Typical Problem

You might have a problem with word order in a sentence you are editing. Consider this sentence:

> In evaluating computer peripherals, our company decided to purchase Brand X's printer.

The writer has not clearly delineated the sequence of events here. The audience may surmise that the "evaluating" came first, or that it occurred at the same time as the purchasing. Grammar handbooks explain that particular tenses indicate the chronological position of events when correct arrangement of information fails to do so. Hence, if the "evaluating" preceded the purchasing—and the word order fails to indicate this—then the sentence should read:

> Our company decided to purchase Brand X's printer after we had evaluated computer peripherals.

The Importance of "Nitpicking"

If you have trouble reconciling this kind of grammatical "nitpicking" with other more "important" matters, remember that "nitpicking" helps the audience read quickly and with increased comprehension. In addition, a grammatically "clean" manuscript presents a professional image for a company. Documents that "work" suggest that a company's products also work.

Available Grammar Handbooks

Any one of the following grammar handbooks will supply answers to knotty problems that arise:

- *The Harper Handbook*, Harper & Row, 1981
- *Harbrace College Handbook*, Harcourt, Brace & World
- *Practical English Handbook*, Houghton Mifflin Company.

Rhetoric Handbooks

Evolution of Rhetorical Handbooks

Traditionally, grammar handbooks have described rhetorical principles. However, today's trend is toward separate texts to describe rhetorical modes, strategies, and figures.

Rhetorical principles underlie persuasive language—the arrangement of language so that it influences the audience in some preordained way. For instance, proposal writers persuasively arrange information by providing an executive summary at the front of a proposal so that decision-makers can understand the features and benefits of the proposal quickly without having to read the entire document. Further, proposal writers fill the executive summary with vertical lists and illustrations.

Throughout the entire proposal, writers repeat the name of their company, their product, and themes they want to communicate. These types of devices, plus crisp phrasing, help persuade the audience.

Two Available Handbooks

The following two handbooks are excellent:

- Lay, Mary. *Strategies for Technical Writing: A Rhetoric With Readings.* New York: Holt, Rinehart, and Winston, 1982.
- Anderson, Steve, and Cox, Don. *The Technical Reader.* New York: Holt, Rinehart, and Winston, 1980.

Military Standards

Definition—Military Standards

Military standards are government publications that dictate special formats and usages. In a sense, military standards are a combination of style manuals, grammar handbooks, and rhetoric handbooks. Defense contractors and others who develop and manufacture goods for the Army, Navy, and Air Force must conform to the rules of written communication contained in these publications. We discussed these military standards in Understand the Requirements, Audience, and Purpose of Documents, Chapter 5.

Twelve Major Errors

The Most Common Errors

Let me offer my list of the most common errors you will encounter in technical manuscripts:

1. Inverted word order
2. Fragments
3. Run-on sentences
4. Ambiguous pronouns (sexist language)
5. Pronouns that fail to agree with their antecedents
6. Subjects that fail to agree with verbs
7. Indiscriminate definition of acronyms and other violations related to use of acronyms
8. Lack of parallelism, especially in a series
9. Comma errors
10. Misuse of the colon in vertical lists, especially after linking verbs
11. Use of the apostrophe
12. Excessive capitalization.

Inverted Word Order

Write Simple Sentences

Since audiences understand information best and most quickly when it is expressed in natural word order—subject, verb, object, write as many sentences as possible to fit this natural word order pattern. Ignore admonitions to create variety in writing by "inverting" the word order of sentences (using introductory words, phrases, and clauses; creating compound and complex sentences). Use as many simple sentences as possible, staying with short words and short sentences and one idea per sentence.

Simplify the Thought

When you encounter a sentence like

> Before you may begin using a system, you must "log on" to it.

revise it to read:

> Log on to a system before using it.

Try It Again

Take a sentence like

> In addition to its command processing functions, another feature of the shell is its programming capability.

and change it to

> The shell has command processing and programming capabilities.

Subject-verb-object word order places the meaning of the sentence closest to the front of the sentence, and audiences grasp meaning best and most quickly when content words are in this position. As far as "variety" is concerned, technical audiences want substance, first and foremost.

> Stop reading now and work through Exercise 17-1 to practice putting sentences in subject-verb-object order.

EXERCISE 17-1 (Individual)

Revise the following five sentences to fit the traditional subject-verb-object sentence pattern.

1. Besides offering outstanding reliability, the system is also extremely cost-effective.

2. Five minutes after receiving AC power, a warm up signal will be received from the transmitter.

3. While providing radar control functions, the RIU also processes video signals.

4. When in test mode and if transmission is not taking place, the RIU generates an STC start pulse.

5. When extinction caused by water and ice particles is accounted for, attenuation at 10 micrometers is much improved.

Fragments

What Is a Fragment?

Fragments are "non-sentences"—that is, they are missing either a subject or verb, or an object necessary to make a sentence complete. Fragments interrupt the audience's concentration and cause it to pause in order to reconstruct meaning.

> Stop reading now and work through Exercise 17-2 to practice rewriting fragments.

**EXERCISE 17-2
(Individual)**

Each of the following five sentences is a fragment. Supply the missing subject, predicate, and/or object.

1. Success achieved even though the project was behind schedule.

2. The method of data collection to be used depends.

3. If the maximum benefit of the PDCS is to be achieved, the ATC must requirements for aircraft separation versus the need for fuel consumption.

4. And tested positively for horizontal stability.

5. Acceptable performance obtained on the single field imagery, though further study might be warranted.

Run-on Sentences

Defining Run-on Sentences

Run-on sentences contain too many ideas in one sentence. As a rule, break long sentences into shorter ones. Look at this long sentence:

> For tactical military operations, the ability to operate in weather will mean the difference between success and failure, and it is clear from figure 2 that operational flying in the European theater will require significant periods of night and adverse weather operations.

Two ideas co-exist in the above sentence: 1) weather will affect the success of missions, and 2) Europe often has hazardous weather. Hence, make it easier on your audience—use just one idea per sentence:

> For tactical military operations, the ability to operate in weather will mean the difference between success and failure. Figure 2 shows that Europe often experiences hazardous weather.

Grammatically, we now have two simple sentences, rather than one run-on sentence.

Hint—Recognizing Run-ons

You can guard against use of run-on sentences and fragments by stabbing one finger at the beginning of a "sentence" and another at the period. This practice exposes exceedingly long sentences and also the usually shorter fragments (discussed on the previous page).

> Stop reading now and work through Exercise 17-3 to practice rewriting run-on sentences.

EXERCISE 17-3 (Individual)

Break the following run-on sentences into simple sentences.

1. The January 4 progress report incorrectly specifies acceptable tracker performance, and the final report on image quality supersedes information from all previous reports.
2. Currently, infrared imagery is obtained using an interlaced scanner, and each image consists of two interlaced fields of 60 rows each.
3. At any instant, several features are being tracked—as required by the growth in feature detail resulting from closure on the feature, the type of tracker may be changed.
4. Dr. James Smith will be the program manager for the proposed program, the principal technical investigator will be Mr. Richard Jones, the lead consultant will be Dr. Donald Brown.

Bare Pronouns

Does It Have an Antecedent?

Every pronoun should be a red flag: stop and find the antecedent of the pronoun. The following two sentences illustrate part of the problem:

> An extension is an optional part of a file name specification, following the filename, separated from it by a period. *It* may have any number of

characters, provided the total number of characters in the filename and extension (including the period) does not exceed 19.

Analyzing the Problem

Which antecedent does *It* refer to? Ranging from the closest possibility (and following the dictum that writers and editors should position antecedents as close to pronouns as possible), is the antecendent. *Period? Filename? Specification? Name? Part? Extension? Extension* is the correct answer, but why force the reader to think through the list of possibilities when simply repeating the noun *Extension* would do the trick?

Another Example

Consider the following passage with the pronouns underscored:

> This technique is now being used in the north sea, and *it* will be interesting to see how *it* works. Our analysis shows *it's* just not cost effective in Gulf of Mexico at shallow depths where divers can be used. However, for deeper platforms where access is by ROV only, *it* may provide an additional and rapid means of checking for flooding and showing that no cracks exceed about 30% of circumference. *It* needs to be compared further to other tools that a ROV can carry for cost effectiveness.

Let's dissect this passage and do a few things quickly just to spruce it up. First, expand the contraction *it's* to *it is* for the sake of the sense of the sentence and for consistency of tone throughout the passage. Next, capitalize *North Sea*, and then substitute the article *an* for *a* in front of *ROV*. Now, consider the major problem of the pronouns:

> This technique is now being used in the North Sea, and *it* will be interesting to see how *it* works.

The antecedent of the second *it* is *technique*, but the first *it* is an expletive. Correctly stated, with an antecedent for all pronouns, you should revise the sentence to read:

> This technique is now being used in the North Sea, and we will watch with interest to see how *it* works.

Solving Additional Problems

Let's examine the subsequent portions of the passage:

> Our analysis shows *it*'s just not cost effective in Gulf of Mexico at shallow depths where divers can be used. However, for deeper platforms where access is by ROV only, *it* may provide an additional and rapid means of checking for flooding and showing that no cracks exceed about 30% of circumference.

The first *it* (*it's*) is an expletive. Even though the second *it* refers to *This technique*, the audience questions the antecedent because of the stretch from this point back to *This technique*. As you revise this passage, substitute *this technique* for the second *it* for the sake of clarity and to ease the burden on the audience.

> Stop reading now and work through Exercise 17-4 to practice substituting nouns for bare pronouns.

EXERCISE 17-4 (Individual)

Substitute nouns for the bare pronouns in the following sentences.

1. The two investigators said the keyboard and terminal failed, so they were scrapped.
2. The system works well in the computer room. However, it often heats up too much.
3. The detector is set into depletion and the read diode is set to its operating potential. This defines the reference level for the voltage-sensing amplifier.
4. This unit is now in the final evaluation stage. It is anticipated that this unit will be used to screen arrays for the program.
5. An on-axis configuration is very compact but requires that a portion of the energy received by the system be blocked or obscured due to the position of a secondary mirror. It impairs system transmission and reduces optical contrast due to diffraction around the obscuration.

Bare Pronouns (Cont.)

Number and Gender

Number refers to singular and plural. Gender refers to feminine and masculine. Pronouns must agree with their antecedents (the words to which pronouns refer) in number and gender.

Spot the Problem

Do you see any problem with this sentence?

> Each of the technicians carried their manual to the meeting.

First, what is the antecedent of the pronoun *their*? Is it *Each* or *technicians*? It isn't *technicians*, for *technicians* is not the subject of the sentence, and *their* refers to the subject. *Each* is a singular pronoun and is the subject of the sentence. The pronoun *their* must agree with its antecedent *Each* in number and gender in order for the sentence to be grammatically correct and professionally acceptable. *Their* fails the test, since it is plural in number. The sentence should read:

> Each of the technicians carried his or her manual to the meeting.

Other Typical Problems

You will encounter other problems in pronoun-antecedent agreement, like ambiguity of reference:

> Corporate executives decided to reject the union's demands because *they* were so unreasonable.

Are the executives unreasonable or are the demands unreasonable? Could be either. The original author taxes the patience of the audience with these ambiguities. The solution to this problem is, again, to repeat the appropriate noun (*executives* or *demands*) rather than using a pronoun.

Sexist Language

Sometimes, I hear men *and* women say that the notion of sexist language is bunk—that using the masculine form of a pronoun should not offend women. "Should" is not the question here. Rather, the fact is that exclusive or excessive use of masculine pronouns does affect some women and men. This fact alone—because we are striving to appeal to our individual audiences—demands that we modify the potentially offensive language. We can appeal to these audiences by

- Changing singular nouns to plural, thereby avoiding the singular pronoun
- Including both the masculine and feminine forms of the pronoun, such as he/she or him/her
- Alternating masculine and feminine forms of the pronoun throughout the manuscript.

> Stop reading now and work through Exercise 17-5 to practice correcting errors in pronoun/antecedent agreement.

EXERCISE 17-5 (Individual)

Correct the pronoun errors in the following sentences.

1. The Engineering Department was proud of their new facilities.
2. Each employee was given his own copy of the manual.
3. The researchers couldn't solve the problems because they didn't conform to normal methodology.
4. The system consists of a terminal and two keyboards; both are manufactured by Digital.
5. The project team was proud of each technician and their contribution to the proposal effort.

Subject-Verb Agreement

Spotting Subject-Verb Agreement Errors

In order to spot subject-verb agreement errors, pick out the subject and predicate in a sentence, and read them together, omitting the qualifying phrases. Do this because lengthy qualifying phrases may cause you to forget what the subject was. For example, look at the following sentence:

> Each of the engineers are responsible for a separate section of the proposal.

When you omit the phrase *of the engineers* you discover that *Each* and *are* don't agree in number.

The sentence should read

Each of the engineers is responsible for a separate section of the proposal.

> Stop reading now and work through Exercise 17-6 to practice working on subject-verb agreement.

EXERCISE 17-6 (Individual)

Correct the errors in subject-verb agreement in the following sentences.

1. A representative sampling of engineers were selected for the proposal effort.
2. When all A1 inputs are high, each of the circuits enter the inputs high output-low state.
3. Extensive analyses is required to provide needed information for project approval.
4. The layout and manufacture of a PWB is costly and time-consuming.
5. Each of the techniques used are effective in producing prototypes.

Acronyms

Guidelines for Using Acronyms

Since so few rules related to use of acronyms exist, I'm taking a shot at creating some guidelines for you:

1. Provide a "List of Abbreviations and Acronyms" in the front matter of technical reports and manuals.
2. Define acronyms the first time they appear in each chapter of a technical manuscript.
3. Pluralize acronyms by adding only "s"—not "'s" or "s'."
4. Use acronyms in headings sparingly.
5. Begin sentences with acronyms sparingly.

Consider a List of Abbreviations and Acronyms

Depending on the audience's technical awareness, you may need a "List of Abbreviations and Acronyms" in the front matter of your document. Even with a highly aware audience, use a "List of Abbreviations and Acronyms" as a guide to these new and shortened groups of letters used as "words."

The following list exemplifies the form for a "List of Abbreviations and Acronyms":

LIST OF ABBREVIATIONS AND ACRONYMS

AC	alternating current
ACU	acquisition control unit
AEDC	after effective date of the contract
ASOS	automated surface observing system
BC/PS	battery charger power supply
CDR	critical design review

The words following each abbreviation and acronym are definitions. The list is alphabetized with a letter-by-letter approach; definitions of the acronyms have no impact on the alphabetization of the acronym itself. Hence AC (alternating current) comes before ACU (acquisition control unit).

Defining Acronyms

Define acronyms the first time they appear in each chapter of a document. This practice reminds readers of the meanings of acronyms each time they encounter an acronym within a chapter. In a very short manuscript, supply a definition for the initial appearance of the acronym in the first chapter only. Once you define the initial acronym in each chapter, the acronym—not the definition—should be used throughout the chapter.

Proper Acronym Format

The correct form for defining initial use of an acronym in the text of a chapter follows:

> This specification describes requirements for a local data acquisition package (DAP) for use in the Automated Surface Observing System (ASOS).

Capitalization of Acronyms

Notice that the first definition in the above example is not capitalized; the second is capitalized because it is the title of the project. Guard against capitalizing definitions that are not proper nouns or proper adjectives. Also, keep in mind that you do not capitalize definitions of acronyms simply because the letters of the acronyms are capitalized.

Pluralization of Acronyms

You can pluralize acronyms in the text, without using an apostrophe:

> The engineer configured the hardware using two DAPs .

However, the "List of Abbreviations and Acronyms" in the front matter should contain only the singular form of the acronym.

Don't Use Acronyms in Headings

Whenever possible, avoid using acronyms in headings of technical reports. Often, audiences will scan a document, reading headings only, and will miss definitions of acronyms.

Beginning a Sentence with an Acronym

You can usually use an acronym to begin a sentence, unless the acronym is the single letter "A," or some other letter that may be mistaken for a word.

Lack of Parallelism

Words Out of Balance

Lack of parallelism means that one or more of the grammatical elements in a sentence do not balance with the other elements.

An Unbalanced Example

What's wrong with the following sentence?

> The instructional designers ordered the following equipment: the TI Business Pro computer, the Toshiba laser printer, the WordStar version 5.0 word processing software, and that later they should order a Smithson optical scanner.

The last element of the series, the one that refers to the optical scanner, doesn't match grammatically with the other elements. The optical scanner element is a subordinate clause, whereas the other elements are noun phrases.

Why Keep Things Parallel?

What's the result of this error? More important than breaking rules of grammar is the fact that the faulty construction distracts the audience from reading the message quickly and clearly. If the sentence had read,

> The instructional designers will order the following equipment: the IBM computer, the Toshiba laser printer, the WordStar version 5.0 word processing software, and, later, a Smithson optical scanner.

then the audience would not have stumbled over the final element of the series. The bottom line with this parallelism problem is the same as with any grammar/usage/mechanics/spelling problem: errors distract the audience from efficiently reading the manuscript.

Other Examples

Faulty parallelism may also occur in other instances:

> The company recruits candidates for employment in data processing, bookkeeping, customer engineers, and sales trainees.

In this sentence, the items in the series are all nouns and noun phrases, but the first two denote occupations and the last two denote persons. Change the sentence to read:

> The company recruits candidates for employment in data processing, bookkeeping, customer service, and sales.

Look at another example.

> Engineers solve problems according to the following process:
> - identify the problem;
> - analyze the problem;
> - the problem should be solved using various techniques and tools;

In this sentence, the first two elements begin with verbs, and the third with an article and then a noun. For the sentence to be parallel, all three elements should begin with verbs, as follows:

- identify the problem;
- analyze the problem;
- develop techniques and tools.

Stop reading now and work through Exercise 17-7 to practice working with parallelism in your documents.

EXERCISE 17-7 (Individual)

Correct errors in parallelism in the following passages.

1. The company is the AI-participant in the program, in which AI, controlling flight, and pilot-vehicle interface technologies are being applied to aid pilots.

2. The QRP 2000 consists of the following:

   - 1 megaword of random-access memory
   - 528 megabytes of on-line high-speed disk storage
   - The system has 48 9600-baud asynchronous terminal ports.
   - This system has an 800/1600 bpi magnetic tape drive.

3. The environment in which this sensor is to work is one with countermeasures, atmospheric obscurants, and includes natural clutter.

4. The proposal team will perform the following tasks:

   - Perform initial study
   - Gather information
   - Outlining
   - Write proposal
   - Organize review sessions
   - Correcting the proposal
   - Coordinate final production.

Comma Errors

Why Worry About Commas?

Comma errors are the most common punctuation errors in most writing. Let's look at a few of the most common comma errors.

Omitting the Comma in a Compound Sentence

Place a comma after the first independent clause and before the coordinating conjunction in a compound sentence. This comma rule consistently causes problems when writers fail to observe it. For example, look at the following example of a compound sentence:

> The software engineer developed the program and the marketing director developed an appropriate sales strategy.

As punctuated, the above sentence tends to run together; a reader may have to look twice to grasp the two related thoughts and the sequence of events. However, by adding a single comma to divide the two clauses, the meaning is much clearer:

> The software engineer developed the program, and the marketing director developed an appropriate sales strategy.

Comma Splices

A comma splice occurs when only a comma separates two independent clauses. A comma splice causes one separate idea to run into another without sufficient warning:

> The oscillator frequency will be 40, 960 cycles per second, this is required to allow the crystal manufacturers a safety margin in meeting vibration requirements for the complete package.

In the above example, the second comma is insufficient to brake the audience's thought process. Rather than the audience biting off one idea after "per second," the audience's grasp for meaning spills over into the second clause. After a time, the audience realizes that he/she has run on into a second thought; the audience must then double back and decide where to break off the first idea. The sentence should correctly read:

> The oscillator frequency will be 40, 960 cycles per second; this is required to allow the crystal manufacturers a safety margin in meeting vibration requirements for the complete package.

A Better Solution

Better yet, the sentence reads:

> The oscillator frequency will be 40, 960 cycles per second; this frequency is required to allow the crystal manufacturers a safety margin in meeting vibration requirements for the complete package.

The use of *frequency* helps avoid a vague pronoun reference. Also, the two clauses may be expressed as two separate sentences. However, because the information in the two independent clauses is so closely allied, use of the semicolon is preferable.

Watch out for comma splices with conjunctive adverbs—words like *however, that is, moreover, further.* Conjunctive adverbs, unlike conjunctions, demand a stronger stop than a comma when they separate two independent clauses. The sentence, "Technical writers write technical prose, and technical editors edit it," is correctly punctuated; however, the sentence, "Technical writers write technical prose, however, technical editors edit it," is not correct. The conjunctive adverb *however* signals a turn in meaning between the two independent clauses (instead of "coordinating" them as *and* does) and demands a semicolon before *however* to avoid misreading.

Commas After Items in a Series

"My teacher said that you had the option of using a comma after the next to last item in a series."

I always wondered why teachers gave this option. Why create ambiguity? To save one small mark of punctuation? There are times when omitting that comma produces ambiguity, such as in the following example:

> She left equal shares of her $100,000,000 estate to Joe, Chuck, Paul, Tony and Pete.

Did she leave four or five equal shares? Without a comma before the *and*, the reader must assume that Tony and Pete each have inherited one-half of one share.

Stop reading now and work through Exercise 17-8 to practice correcting comma splices.

EXERCISE 17-8 (Individual)

Correct the comma errors in the following constructions.

1. The project was completed successfully and the system was implemented into production.
2. A smaller area is available for the CCD and it integrates 8 times more in the chip, thus the CCD dynamic range is 69 dB and the CIM has 91 dB dynamic range.
3. The consultant recommended periodic maintenance on the keyboard, terminal and disk drive.
4. The two possible effects are an increased mirror size, and a decrease in scan efficiency.
5. Use of a common afocal (whether reflective, refractive or a hybrid), will allow for a single scan mirror to scan the scene.

Use of the Apostrophe

Rules for Using Apostrophes

Many writers leave out the apostrophe entirely rather than deal with it. You should insert apostrophes in the following places:

*   Between the last letter of the noun and the final "s" to show possession, e.g., IBM's new computer
*   After the final "s" to show plural possession, e.g., engineers' writing skills
*   Between the letter or number and the "s" to show quantity—e.g., too many "y's" in the spelling of that word, or too many "5's" in that equation. However, do not use an apostrophe in the same situation involving an acronym—e.g., too many BARs (Base Address Registers).

> Stop reading now and work through Exercise 17-9 to
> practice correcting apostrophe errors.

**EXERCISE 17-9
(Individual)**

Correct the apostrophe errors in the following sentences.

1. When the FCCs failed, pilots had to take manual control of the aircraft.
2. The consultants recommended switching to another manufacturer's system, such as NECs system.
3. The subsidiaries profits failed to meet established corporate goals.
4. A screen full of 5s indicates a failed test.
5. EM/OSs powerful electronic mail capabilities allow it to provide inter-office communication between all the corporations PC's.

**Excessive
Capitalization**

A Few Rules for Capitalization

Although it is proper to capitalize the name of specific equipment like the Temperature Datum Amplifier, it is *not* proper to capitalize the names of parts of equipment when these parts are common nouns. A good rule to follow is this: When in doubt, do not capitalize.

Check Your Capitalization IQ

Technical writing requires no special rules for capitalization. Follow conventional usage: capitalize proper nouns and proper adjectives. With this generalization as a standard, ask yourself whether or not the italic constructions are proper nouns or proper adjectives and, therefore, deserving of an initial capital letter:

1. Refer to *figure 2* and *table 2* to discover data relevant to the problem.
2. John is a *software systems engineer* who works in the *engineering training branch*.
3. My *manager* asked if I would bring in evidence certifying the *bachelor's* and *master's* degrees I have earned.

Analyzing the Samples

In example 1, neither *figure* nor *table* is a proper noun. According to 3.9 in the *Government Printing Office Style Manual* (1984):

> A common noun used with a date, number, or letter, merely to denote time or sequence, or for the purpose of reference, record, or temporary convenience, does not form a proper name and is therefore not capitalized.

In example 2, *software systems engineer* is a job description—in the same sense that attorney, doctor, and clerk are—and not a title. On the other hand, *Engineering Training Branch* deserves capital letters because it is a principal administrative division.

In example 3, *manager* is another job description and *bachelor's* and *master's* are common nouns describing general—not specific—degrees.

Computer Support

Evolution of Computer-Based Revision Tools

The first computer-based writing and revising tools concentrated on mechanics. Computers follow rules. Use of computers to check execution of rules was an obvious and logical step. Thus, we were presented with spelling checkers. In a spell check program, the computer simply compares each word with a dictionary and reports any failure to locate a word. Hyphenation also was a candidate for checking either by referring to a dictionary or by following a set of rules (called hyphenation algorithms). More and more text manipulations were automated, and now the computer contributes to the art, composition, and printing functions.

The computer is a solid citizen in the publishing community, and the impact of computers in publishing is growing at a pace that defies description. The following paragraphs provide only a peek into a few computer capabilities that can be classified as writer's tools. Machines and the software are growing and improving so rapidly that any attempt at a comprehensive description would be obsolete before publication.

Then how do you keep up? Magazines and manufacturers' sales literature probably offer the best opportunities.

Capabilities of Spelling Checkers

Spelling checkers offer a broad range of capabilities. The comparison checkers mentioned previously simply report that no incorrect words were found or point to words not found in the look-up dictionary. More sophisticated spelling checkers offer alternative words for each word not found in the look-up dictionary. Some checkers offer alternatives based on similar spelling, similar spelling plus word length, or even phonetically similar words. In most cases when an alternative list is offered, you can select the properly spelled word, and the correct word is immediately substituted for the incorrect word.

Most spelling checkers permit new words, including proper names, to be added to the look-up dictionary so that technical words unique to a particular organization are not flagged as unknown by the spelling checker. Modern, built-in, look-up dictionaries typically contain more than 100,000 words.

An Excellent Time-Saver

The spelling checker is an excellent writer's tool. Even the least sophisticated checker will locate typographical errors such as omitted letters, inverted letters, and gibberish created when the typist's hands are temporarily on the wrong keyboard area. If you have access to an automated spelling checker, use it on every document. The check is rapid and efficient. Typographical errors make a document appear amateurish and indicate a lack of craftsmanship.

Some checkers detect double words; that is, a word typed twice. Double word errors most often occur with one word at the end of one line of text and the duplicate appearance at the beginning of the next line. These double words are particularly difficult for a human proofreader to detect.

Limitations of Spell Checkers

Every tool has limitations. "Every spelling program represents a vain attempt to impose the clarity and logic of machine language on the disorder and ambiguities of human language." [PC Magazine, Vol 6, No. 17, 13 October 1987, pg 349.]

Spelling checkers, for instance, will not locate a word that is spelled correctly but used improperly. Some example possibilities of faulty usage are

Accent/ascent/assent	Disburse/Disperse
Accept/Except	Elapse/Lapse
Adapt/Adept/Adopt	Eminent/Imminent
Adverse/Averse	Envelop/Envelope
Advice/Advise	Farther/Further
Affect/Effect	Fewer/Less
All right/Alright	Forward/Foreword
Allusion/Illusion/Delusion	Imply/Infer
Alternate/Alternative	Its/It's
Altogether/All together	Later/Latter
Anyone/Any one	Lay/Laid
Assure/Insure/Ensure	Lie/Lay/Lain
Biannually/Biennially	Maybe/May be
Bimonthly/Semimonthly	Practical/Practicable
Can/May	Precedence/Precedents
Capital/Capitol	Principal/Principle
Carat/Caret/Karat	Raise/Raised
Cite/Sight/Site	Respectfully/Respectively
Complement/Compliment	Stationary/Stationery
Comprise/Compose	Than/Then
Continual/Continuous	To/Too/Two
Council/Counsel/Consul	Toward/Towards
Credible/Creditable/	Who/Whom
Credulous	Who's/Whose
Discreet/Discrete	Your/You're
Disinterested/Uninterested	

Still Room for Human Involvement

Spelling checkers don't detect words that are inadvertently omitted. And a "little" word like *not* omitted from a legal document is too important to trust to automation.

A spell checker dictionary that contains the single letter "b" will not detect the typographical error when the typist leaves the second letter off the word *be.* Again, use your spelling checker on every document. But be aware of the limitations as well as the capabilities. Take advantage of the capabilities and use your human abilities to overcome the shortcomings.

Thesauruses

Thesauruses show alternate definitions for individual words and suggest synonyms. These on-line thesauruses are convenient and more thorough than most printed versions, because the alternate definitions are shown on a single screen; hence, you don't have to look at several places in a printed thesaurus. On-line thesauruses typically contain 200,000 words or more.

Like spelling checkers, thesauruses vary widely in quality.

Grammar Checkers

The broad category of grammar checkers includes software packages with a number of capabilities. The most common functions are passive voice detection, sexism detection, unbalanced marks, and preposition count.

Passive voice detectors locate each use of the verb "to be." Sexism detectors locate single-sex words (his, he, etc.). These tools can help locate a passive voice or sexist use that you missed.

A preposition count is informative in conjunction with a total word count. Prepositions normally account for between 8 percent and 10 percent of the words in text. Any percentage larger than 10 indicates probable over-use of prepositions.

Limitations of Grammar Checkers

Grammar checkers are powerful tools and help overcome some very real human shortcomings. But again, they are only tools. They can show a possible problem, but they cannot correct the problem. Rightly so. A problem might not exist. Passive voice is usually inefficient, and the text should usually be rewritten in active voice. Sexist words in our modern society are frequently offensive. But not always. Human judgment is required. Passive voice might be the perfect choice in a particular situation. A single gender word is not necessarily offensive to either sex. Many grammar checkers will identify words such as *craftsman* or *workman* as single-sex words, but those words are not offensive to most people.

Proofread Your Own Documents

The Need for Proofreading

A document tainted with smudges, misspellings, and typos reflects badly on you, as do errors in grammar, usage, and mechanics.

Do not proofread when you are fatigued or hurried. Also, try not to proofread after you have been revising the same manuscript for an extended period of time. If you do, you may see things that aren't there, and you may not see things that are there.

Get Help to Proofread

Ask a colleague to assist you. Turn the manuscript over to the colleague and have him/her read it with "fresh eyes." Someone who hasn't worked with the manuscript will see the errors more clearly than you will.

You may also read the manuscript aloud to a colleague. Any errors will surface as you read deliberately to an audience. This method differs from your reading the document aloud to yourself. Without an audience, you may tend to hurry or to skip confidently through passages that you "know."

If You Proofread on Your Own . . .

If circumstances force you to proofread on your own, be sure to

1. Run through the entire manuscript, verifying correct pagination. Run through again, verifying the proper numbering of figures. Then do the same for tables. Accomplish these three tasks—pagination, figures, and tables—discretely rather than trying to accomplish each task in one reading.

2. Size up each page. "Eyeball" the page; make sure that it is balanced, that the format remains the same as it was on the previous page.

3. Read all the headings, subheadings, and action titles before reading the text. Verify the logical movement from one heading to another. Verify uniform spelling and use of words from one heading to another.

4. Now start reading the text. Use the reading dynamics technique described in Chapter 6—sweep your hand under each line of text with your editing pen lodged in the fingers of your sweep hand. You're not really reading at this point; rather, you are looking for errors. Looking rather than reading allows you to move rapidly over the page. Remember, you have read this material at least once and maybe even two or three times before. You don't need to read it again.

In sweeping across the pages, you will discover typos, misspellings, redundant words and phrases, undefined acronyms, overdefined acronyms, excessive capitals, and missing punctuation. Your proofreading efforts will clean the manuscript up nicely and ensure its professional look.

> Stop reading now and work through Exercises 17-10 and 17-11 to put together some of the lessons you have learned in Part 4.

EXERCISE 17-10 (Individual)

Refer to Exercise 12-1.

Identify all errors in grammar, usage, spelling, and mechanics in the two "write as you speak" sections of your Writing Sample. Use proofreaders' marks to indicate violations. For instance, place carets where commas and other punctuation marks belong and circle incorrect punctuation marks. Put a slash mark through unnecessary capital letters. (Consult any dictionary or style manual for a complete list of proofreaders' marks.)

**EXERCISE 17-11
(Individual)**

Refer to Exercise 12-1.

Now that you have identified passive voice, weak verbs, jargon, redundancy, unnecessary words, grammar, usage, spelling, and mechanics errors, revise the two "write as you speak" sections of your Writing Sample.

Do not attempt to revise on your transcription sheets. Begin anew on a clean sheet of paper.

This exercise completes your work with the Writing Sample for the purposes of this book.

The Bottom Line

A Product You Can Be Proud Of

Armed with a foreknowledge of major errors in technical documents and the means to correct them, you can correct the problems that result in unprofessional appearing documents. Remember to

- Strive for consistency and correctness.
- Consult appropriate manuals and handbooks when questions arise.
- Become familiar with the most common documentation errors and work to prevent them.

INDEX